Israel in the plan of God

Israel in the plan of God

Light on today's debate

Steve Motyer

Inter-Varsity Press

INTER-VARSITY PRESS
38 De Montfort Street, Leicester LE1 7GP, England

First published 1989, 1991

British Library Cataloguing in Publication Data

Motyer, Stephen, *1950–*
Israel in the plan of God.
1. Bible. Special subjects: Israel.
Theological aspects
I. Title
220.8′933

ISBN 0–85110–671–4

Set in 10.5/12 pt Baskerville by
Input Typesetting Ltd, London
Printed in Great Britain by
Cox & Wyman Ltd, Reading, Berkshire

*Inter-Varsity Press is the book-publishing division of the Universities and
Colleges Christian Fellowship (formerly the Inter-Varsity Fellowship), a student
movement linking Christian Unions in universities and colleges throughout the
United Kingdom and the Republic of Ireland, and a member movement of the
International Fellowship of Evangelical Students. For information about local and
national activities write to UCCF, 38 De Montfort Street, Leicester LE1 7GP.*

Contents

Preface

I have been living with Romans 9 – 11 for many years; since undergraduate days, in fact, when the teasing quality of these chapters first caught my imagination and I started to wrestle with them. Since then, my understanding of them has undergone many a change, and doubtless will yet. But the fascination of them has never waned, and with each fresh study new insights have emerged and the living word of the apostle has gripped me anew.

Any Christian who wants to think through the Christian attitude towards the Jews today must come to terms with Romans 9 – 11. Yet I am convinced that these chapters have frequently been misunderstood. The trouble is the old one of taking out of their context verses whose meaning seems to be obvious – when in fact their meaning grows out of the context in which they are set. So the theory on which this book rests is that we cannot rightly understand Romans 11:26, 'all Israel will be saved', unless we look at the whole sweep of Paul's argument in these three chapters, and the setting of these chapters in his whole ministry.

Because my thinking about these chapters has been gently brewing for so long, I owe a debt of gratitude to many people of whom I am no longer aware. I am especially grateful to Tom Wright for many invaluable stimuli in the distant past, and for reading and commenting most helpfully on the whole manuscript. I also want to record my thanks to David Harley and Walter Riggans of All Nations Christian College, and to Sister Margaret Shepherd of the Sisters of Sion Study Centre in London, for her prompt kindness in helping me gain insight into the work of her Congregation.

Finally, of course, my deepest thanks go to my wife for her

encouragement and patience, and it is to her that I dedicate this book, with the prayer that God may use it to his glory.

Steve Motyer

CHAPTER ONE

God's people for ever?

Israel is in the news – a constant object of media attention. But media interest has been matched in recent years by a growing interest among Christians, at all levels. Reasons for this are not hard to find.

Some Christian circles have long given Israel a special place in God's plan. But at a popular level this has been strongly reinforced by influential writers like Hal Lindsey, who have encouraged Christians to see biblical prophecy being fulfilled in the Middle East today.[1] The re-establishment of the State of Israel in 1948 has been understood by many as God's sign of his continuing concern for the Jews. This has naturally generated great excitement, which continues unabated. Recent years have also seen an increase in the number of 'messianic' congregations of Jews who combine Christian faith with a continuing commitment to their Jewish heritage.

It is the same at a theological level. The spectre of the Holocaust in Europe during the second world war, when six million Jews were exterminated by the Nazis, haunts theologians today. The problem is that Christianity cannot escape a share of the blame for that awful atrocity. It took place in a country shaped by a church whose founder called synagogues 'nothing but a den of devils' and who urged Christians to 'set fire to their synagogues or schools . . . I advise that their

---

[1] Hal Lindsey, *The Late Great Planet Earth* (Zondervan, 1970). My copy proclaims, 'Over 1,600,000 copies in print'. Another book which has been very widely circulated is that of Wilbur M. Smith, *Arab/Israeli Conflict and the Bible* (Regal Books, 1967).

houses also be razed and destroyed . . . eject them forever from the country . . . be on your guard against the Jews and avoid them so far as possible'.[2] These awful words of Martin Luther fuelled cruelty against the Jews in Germany right up to the atrocities of the Hitler era, and form a terrible blot on Christian history. It is not surprising, therefore, that theologians continue to discuss the Holocaust, trying to determine the appropriate Christian response.

And likewise, on the ecclesiastical level, there has been a growth of concern and interest. The last twenty years have seen a series of official pronouncements from various church bodies, all aimed at defining the Christian attitude towards the Jews and Judaism in the post-Holocaust era. These statements all arise from a deep sense of guilt at Christian injustices against the Jews, and from a heartfelt desire to change direction in our relationship with them.

It must be a step forward, to replace negligence or hostility with respect and concern. But sadly there is little agreement about the form which Christian respect and concern for the Jews should take. How far should we go, in seeking to make amends for the wrongs of the past? Some theologians are arguing that we must change our entire understanding of Jesus because of the Holocaust. Even though the Holocaust was not perpetrated by believers, they say, it could only have taken place within the atmosphere of confrontation and rejection which has sadly always existed between Christians and Jews, and which is ultimately caused by Christianity's exclusive claim for itself. The Roman Catholic theologian Gregory Baum, for instance, argues that 'anti-Jewish ideology is finally lodged in the Church's central dogma regarding Jesus Christ', because simply saying that Jesus is the only Saviour 'ultimately removes Israel from a place in the sun'. And so we need to revise the exclusive claim made in the New Testament itself, he suggests, and adopt a theology 'that does not make Jesus the messiah of Israel who fulfils

---

[2] Martin Luther, *On the Jews and Their Lies* (1543), published in *Luther's Works*, vol. 47 (Fortress, 1971), quotations from pp. 172, 268, 269, 274.

all the divine promises'.[3]

But biblical Christians will feel great reluctance to go this far. It is undeniably true that the Holocaust must change our attitude to Jews for ever: but does it really mean that we must give up the heart of our own faith? In any case, can the New Testament authors really be blamed for the excesses of later history? Some of their statements do indeed sound thoroughly anti-Semitic when we read them today. In John's Gospel, Jesus accuses 'the Jews' of belonging 'to your father, the devil' (8:44), and Paul does not hesitate to quote one of the 'cursing' psalms and apply it to Israel: 'May their table become a snare and a trap, a stumbling-block and a retribution . . . May their eyes be darkened so they cannot see, and their backs be bent for ever' (Rom. 11:9–10, quoting Ps. 69:22–23).

Translated into our world today, we cannot imagine taking such language on our lips. But is it fair to judge the New Testament authors by modern conditions? They were living and writing in very different circumstances. We want to understand them on their own terms, because only so can we really hear what they have to say to us today. Perhaps the problem arises partly from the fact that verses like these have been plucked out of their context, without asking (for instance) to whom precisely John was referring as 'the Jews'. Did he really mean 'all descendants of Abraham', or is 'the Jews' just shorthand for 'Jesus' enemies' in John 8?

That brings us to the purpose of this book. In the rest of this chapter, we will survey briefly some of the popular, theological and ecclesiastical developments mentioned above, and then jump back into the early church, to trace the roots of the present situation. In chapter 2, we will focus on Paul, looking at the way in which he faced similar issues in his own ministry. Then with chapter 3 we will begin on the main project of the book: a close look at the section of the letter to the Romans from which the quotation above is taken. What exactly led Paul to write like that? Romans 9 – 11 is a closely

---

[3] Gregory Baum, 'Catholic Dogma After Auschwitz', in A. T. Davies (ed.), *Anti-semitism and the Foundations of Christianity* (Paulist Press, 1979), pp. 137–150. Quotations from pp. 144, 146, 147.

packed argument that needs to be seen as a whole before the meaning of each part can be properly appreciated. Finally (chapter 15) we will come back to the present and draw conclusions for today.

This means that our aim is limited. As soon as we begin to reflect on relations between Jews and Christians many issues are raised, but we cannot hope to touch on them all. We are going right back to basics, to look again at one of the central New Testament passages that bears upon the whole question, with the aim simply of letting Paul speak, clearly and authentically, from his own situation to ours.

Popular developments

Recent years have seen remarkable changes in Christian attitudes towards Jews. While some groups continue to promote evangelistic missionary activity among them, others have rejected this idea completely. This change has taken place in widely different groups. Among Catholics, we can see it most clearly in the Sisters of Sion, who began life as a missionary order in the nineteenth century, but are now totally opposed to evangelism, teaching that Jews have their own viable way to God apart from Christ. They concentrate their ministry instead on humanitarian work among Jews world-wide, and on promoting reconciliation between Christians and Jews through education. They aim simply to be 'a presence of openness and service' towards Jews (and indeed to all). This remarkable change has taken place just since the second world war.[4]

At the other end of the church spectrum, we can point to the International Christian Embassy in Jerusalem, which likewise rejects the idea of evangelizing Jews, but takes its inspiration and support from American fundamentalism. It has 'chapters' in many cities in the United States. It too seeks to be an expression of Christian support and solidarity with

---

[4] A helpful summary of the history of the Sisters of Sion, and of their development to their present position, is provided by Charlotte Klein, 'From Conversion to Dialogue – the Sisters of Sion and the Jews: a Paradigm of Catholic–Jewish Relations?', *Journal of Ecumenical Studies* 18 (1981), pp. 388–400.

Israel, and undertakes humanitarian projects in Israel as a ministry of 'comfort', in obedience to Isaiah 40:1.[5]

At a popular level, dispensationalists have long given Israel a special place in God's plan for the world. They believe that the millennium, the thousand-year reign of Christ on earth following his return, will be centred on Jerusalem, and that the Old Testament prophecies of the blessing of Israel in the promised land will be literally fulfilled at that time. At the moment we live in the age (or 'dispensation') of the church, in which the world-wide people of God is being formed. But when the millennium comes, this dispensation will end, and Israel will once again take her place at centre-stage. Meanwhile, the perceptive Christian discerns the hand of the Lord in the formation of the Israeli State: 'It constitutes a preparation for the end of the age, the setting for the coming of the Lord for His Church, and the fulfilment of Israel's prophetic destiny.'[6]

There are many varieties and shades of dispensationalism. In Britain, it has never been as influential as in the United States, but there are nevertheless many Christian groups who adopt a 'dispensationalist' outlook to the extent that they see the fulfilment of Old Testament prophecy in the political re-establishment of Israel and feel themselves committed as Christians to Israel's well-being. Within the Reformed tradition in Britain, a belief in the centrality of Israel in God's plan goes right back to the 16th century, and this tradition exercises its influence still. The growing numbers and influence of 'messianic' Jews have contributed to keeping the issue in the forefront of church life.[7]

---

[5] There is both a critique and defence of the work and aims of the Embassy in the *Bulletin of the Lausanne Consultation on Jewish Evangelism*, Issue 7, pp. 2–11.

[6] John F. Walvoord, *Israel in Prophecy* (Zondervan, 1962), p. 26. This book well represents the full-blown dispensationalist view of Israel.

[7] A moderate dispensationalism of this sort is represented by Daniel C. Juster, 'Covenant and Dispensation: Towards a Messianic Jewish Perspective', *Mishkan* 2 (1985), pp. 24–42; also John Fischer, *The Olive Tree Connection: Sharing Messiah with Israel* (IVP, Downers Grove, 1983); and (writing within the Reformed tradition) Erroll Hulse, *The Restoration of Israel* (Henry E. Walter, 1971). Iain Murray helpfully shows how central the belief in the restoration of Israel was in Reformed theology in *The Puritan Hope* (Banner of Truth, 1971), pp. 37–82.

Ecclesiastical developments

These 'grass-roots' changes have been matched by the official pronouncements of several churches. Gregory Baum under-lines the change in Catholic teaching at the Second Vatican Council: instead of teaching that the Jews collectively bear the guilt of the crucifixion, the Roman Catholic church now teaches 'that the Jewish people continue to be God's chosen people, that their religion remains for them a source of divine grace, and that it is the task of Christians to engage in conver-sation and cooperation with them'.[8]

Other official bodies have followed suit. In January 1980 the General Synod of the Protestant Church in the Rheinland, West Germany, passed a declaration affirming 'the permanent election of the Jewish people as the people of God', and according Israel a continuing unique status in God's purposes for the world. Three months later the German Roman Cath-olic bishops issued a long statement, maintaining essentially the same position. And in May 1981 the General Assembly of the Church of Scotland declared its 'belief in the continuing place of God's people Israel within the divine purpose', in response to a report of its Overseas Council, which begins with the striking statement, 'Jews cannot be treated by Chris-tians as unbelievers but only as brother believers with whom they are privileged to share a common faith in God, and the same promises of salvation.'[9]

In this way a popular and theological commitment to Israel is becoming accepted by some of the mainstream churches.

Theological developments

Behind official statements like these lies the work of many

---

[8] Baum, 'Catholic Dogma', p. 137. This is his summary of the teaching of Vatican II. Interestingly, he feels that this is already a considerable advance on the teaching of the New Testament. Pope John Paul II, addressing Jewish leaders in Mainz on 17th November 1980, spoke of the Jews as 'the people of God of the Old Covenant, which has never been revoked by God'.

[9] These three statements are usefully published as appendices in D. W. Tor-rance (ed.), *The Witness of the Jews to God* (Handsel Press, 1982).

theologians, who are often the pioneers of new ideas long before they percolate down to grassroots level. In fact theologians have been thinking very radical thoughts in this area. Very important is the name of Rosemary Radford Ruether, whose book *Faith and Fratricide* has set out the agenda for subsequent discussion. Responding to the challenge of the Holocaust, she argues forcibly that the New Testament and Christian theology misinterpreted Jesus' proclamation of the kingdom of God, making it imply a rejection of the Old Testament and of Judaism – and that Paul was one of the chief culprits in this. Paul's rejection of the Old Testament law, she argues, was based on a 'fatal distortion' of the way the law was actually understood by Jews, and created the subsequent hostility between the two religions. She too proposes that we must alter our understanding of Jesus, so that we do not understand him to be the final revelation of God's kingdom.[10]

New Testament scholars, and particularly specialists in Paul, have not been slow to take up her challenge. Two in particular deserve mention. Lloyd Gaston and John Gager have both tried to vindicate Paul from the charge that he rejected the law. In fact, they argue, Paul did no such thing. He remained faithful to the religion of the Old Testament, and never taught that Jews had to believe in Jesus in order to be saved. Some of them – like Paul himself – might come to faith in Christ, but they could equally well be saved by the faith that Abraham had, under the 'old covenant'. For Paul, say Gaston and Gager, Christ was simply God's way of bringing Gentiles into the covenant alongside Jews. However, they agree with Ruether about the distortions introduced by later theologians: they think that they are the first to rediscover the true Paul, after centuries of misinterpretation in which he has been taken to reject Judaism and the law.[11]

---

[10] R. R. Ruether, *Faith and Fratricide, The Theological Roots of Anti-Semitism* (Seabury, 1974).

[11] Lloyd Gaston, 'Paul and the Torah', in A. T. Davies (ed.), *Antisemitism and the Foundations of Christianity* (Paulist Press, 1979), pp. 48–71; also 'Israel's Enemies in Pauline Theology', *New Testament Studies* 28 (1982), pp. 400–423: John G. Gager, *The Origins of Anti-Semitism* (OUP, 1983), pp. 193–264.

One more name is worth mentioning: a very different scholar, and one more in tune with the 'popular' and 'official' side of things, but a very eminent theologian nonetheless. Professor T. F. Torrance is a former Moderator of the Church of Scotland, and author of the Overseas Council Report quoted above. He describes Israel in these terms: 'As the appointed instrument of God's self-communication and self-commitment to humanity, Israel constitutes the critical centre in the human race . . . it must be pointed out that any breach . . . with Israel would mean a breaking away from the centre of God's order of redemptive recreation and reunification of mankind.' By 'Israel' he means the Jewish people, not the Israeli State. He underlines the tragedy of Christian neglect of the Jews: 'The deepest schism in the one People of God is the schism between the Christian and the Jewish Church, not that between East and West or Roman and Protestant Christianity.'[12]

One's immediate reaction to statements like these is that they ascribe to Israel the position which Paul reserves for Christ. Indeed, Torrance draws a parallel between Israel and Jesus in order to come to terms with the Holocaust: in this atrocity we see messianic suffering, Israel fulfilling her calling to be the suffering Servant of the Lord, so that she and Christ are 'for ever forged together in a new and quite irreversible way'.[13]

'Israel theology'

We have surveyed a wide range of views, varying greatly from each other. Contemporary Christian thinking about Israel amounts to a confusing clamour of voices, so that it is hardly surprising if we end up uncertain what we should believe. But it is interesting that, amid all the variety, there is one strand which is consistently there in all these positions – the belief that the Jews are 'God's people for ever'. The variety appears

---

[12] T. F. Torrance, 'The divine vocation and destiny of Israel in world history', in D. W. Torrance (ed.), *The Witness of the Jews to God* (Handsel Press, 1982), pp. 85–104. Quotations from pp. 86, 87, 92.

[13] Art. cit., p. 96.

in the different ways in which Jesus is related to this common belief. At one end of the spectrum, there are those who argue that he simply provides a second way of salvation, alongside the Jewish way; at the other, those who simply expect a future conversion of Israel to faith in Christ. The line that holds the spectrum together is this conviction, that Israel has not ceased to be 'God's people' because of the coming of Christ.

Our purpose in this book is not to assess each position individually, but to silence the clamour for a while and listen intently to Paul. As we do so, we shall cast an occasional side-glance at the contemporary debate, and particularly at this 'Israel theology' (as I shall call it) which underlies all these various viewpoints.

Repairing an age-old breach

We must certainly repair breaches and repent of the awful way that Christians have treated Jews down through the centuries. But how far back should our repentance go? The breach between Christianity and Judaism goes back to the eve of the Jewish War of AD 67–73. For there came a moment when (according to the Christian historian Eusebius), the Christians in Jerusalem took the deliberate decision not to stand by their fellow-Jews to defend the city against the advancing Roman armies, but instead broke away from 'the centre of God's order of redemptive recreation' (see above), and left *en masse*.[14]

Should they have stayed to express their solidarity in the one people of God? Does our repentance need to go back this far? Before that date, there had certainly been tensions between Christians and Jews, but nothing that amounted to a final breach. Indeed, particularly in Jerusalem, there were many Christians who simply incorporated their new faith into their previous Jewish life-style (*e.g.* Acts 21:20).

---

[14] Eusebius, *Ecclesiastical History* iii. 5.3. Some have pointed to the relevance of Jesus' command in Mark 13:14, 'When you see the "abomination of desolation" standing where it should not . . . then let those who are in Judea flee to the mountains', and wondered whether the Christians could have been motivated by it in their flight from Jerusalem.

It was that dreadful six-year war with the Romans which made the difference. Comparison with the Holocaust is not inappropriate, for the Romans were absolutely ruthless in their treatment of the Jews. So far as we can tell, Jewish Christians had always refused to support 'zealot' – that is, guerrilla – activity against the Roman occupying forces. But when the war loomed, they could no longer sit on the sidelines, for the Romans would make no distinction between Jews and Christians when they lined the population up for crucifixion. How deep did their commitment to Judaism go? The Jerusalem Christians decided that obedience to Christ did not require them to die in a hopeless defence of the city. So they fled.

Within years of the end of the war, curses on the Christians were introduced into the regular synagogue prayers. There was no going back.

We need to come to terms with this past. In our century, too, Christians failed to stand by Israel in her hour of need. We need to ask, what were the influences which led these pious Jews so to abandon the Holy City at that desperate moment? As we seek to analyse what these may have been, one name presents itself as more important than any other – that of the apostle Paul. It was he who taught the church to regard itself as separate from Judaism. Gaston and Gager doubt it, but really it is indisputable, as we shall see: had he been there, Paul would have marched at the head of the column, as the Christians left Jerusalem that day. Indeed, he had mentally and physically left Jerusalem long before that date.

It is to Paul that we need to turn, as we seek the *theological reasons* for the age-long breach between Christianity and Judaism. We will not find in him any justification for the failure of Christians to love and support the Jews when they have been hated and persecuted – certainly nothing to justify the Christians' own hatred of them. But we will find the reasons which led him and, finally, the whole church to think of Christianity as a different religion – and in the light of them we will be better able to assess the views we have surveyed.

CHAPTER TWO

Paul and Israel: setting the scene

We start by returning to the question raised in chapter one. We can put it simply, as we did then: Are the Jews still the chosen people of God? Or we can express it more theologically, like this: What effect did the coming of Christ have on the old covenant promises made to Israel? Then we can elaborate it, dividing it into separate questions:

1. Were the old covenant promises of such a sort that nothing could change them – not even the coming of the Messiah?

2. Does unbelief exclude Israelites from the orbit of covenant blessings? If not, what effect does it have? (Is it possible for Israel to enjoy a status – chosen, special – which can be lost by individual Jews?)

3. What about non-Jews – on what conditions could they be brought in to enjoy the covenant blessings of the Old Testament? Do these conditions still apply, when they seek now to enjoy the blessings of the Messiah?

4. What about the Old Testament law? If the Old Testament still stands, should followers of the Messiah still be observing (for instance) circumcision and the food laws?

5. If the Old Testament still stands in its own right, is faith in the Messiah to some extent optional? Putting it another way, can Jews still be 'saved' under old covenant grace, without faith in the Messiah? If not, then in what sense does the Old Testament still have validity as the Word of God? Is its validity destroyed?

All these questions are hidden underneath the simple-sounding enquiry, Are the Jews still the people of God? One of the problems we face is that the literature proposing the 'Israel theology' outlined in the last chapter draws a decent veil over many of these further ramifications. For instance, it makes an unspoken distinction between the Old Testament covenant (which continues uninterrupted after Christ) and the Old Testament law (in many points abrogated by Christ). The proponents of this viewpoint would not dream of suggesting that Christians, whether of Jewish or Gentile stock, should circumcise their children according to the law of Moses. But why not? A good reason has to be found why one part of God's Word – his covenant promises to Israel – continues, while another part, his covenant law to Israel, is set aside. In the Old Testament itself, these are one whole package.

Perhaps we need to repent of more than just a false attitude towards Israel, and follow the example of Joshua who, when he realized that circumcision had been neglected all through the period of wilderness wandering, administered it to the entire nation on the verge of the Promised Land (Jos. 5:1–9). In fact all these questions boil down to one. Why did Jesus tell his disciples to baptize the disciples they were to make of all nations, and not to circumcise them (Mt. 28:19)?

Trouble in the early church

The earliest Christians were far more aware than some of today's 'Israel' theologians of the range of problems raised in relating the Old to the New. They wrestled with all the questions listed above. In fact, it would not be putting it too strongly to say that these theological questions shaped Paul's whole ministry, as he sought to argue for his understanding of the answer to them, over against those who answered them differently. The argument became very sharp – in fact, the early church nearly sundered because of it, although Paul did his utmost to hold the two sides together while insisting that he was right.

According to Acts, it was Stephen who first felt that Jesus had come to do more than just reform Israel. But as soon as he suggested that, because of Jesus, the temple could no longer be the focus of God's presence on earth, he provoked a violent response that caused his own death (Acts 6:8 – 7:60). This idea was rejected, not only by Jews, but also by other Jewish Christians, for, as a general rule they carried on with all their customary observances – worshipping in the miracles performed among them (Acts 5:12; *etc.*), their public gatherings in the temple, attending the feasts and festivals, circumcising their children. Followers of 'the Way', as they were known, were distinctive only for their enthusiasm and boldness (Acts 2:46; 4:31), their care for the weak and poor (Acts 4:34; 6:1f.), the miracles performed among them (Acts 5:12; *etc.*), their public gatherings in the temple (Acts 2:46; 5:12), and above all for their proclamation of Jesus the Messiah (Acts 2:36; 4:10; 4:33; *etc.*). They were not distinctive for their violations of the law – except in that they insisted on regarding as Messiah one who had been executed as a criminal, and whom the law therefore called 'cursed' (Dt. 21:23). That alone brought them into conflict with the religious authorities (Acts 4:1–3; 5:17ff.).

But then, as the story unfolds in Acts, we reach the moment (Acts 10) when Peter, dozing on the roof of Simon the tanner's house, suddenly received a heavenly vision to the effect that he 'should not call any man impure or unclean' (Acts 10:9–16, 28). Then he found himself whisked off into the home of a pious Gentile, on whom the Holy Spirit fell as Peter preached. Stunned at this lack of discrimination on the part of the Holy Spirit, Peter felt compelled to baptize Cornelius, and then – horror of horrors – to accept table hospitality from him (Acts 10:47f.).

It is hard for us to enter into the shocking nature of Peter's action: but perhaps it becomes a little clearer when we reflect that, in all likelihood, his visit to Cornelius marked the first occasion when he had ever entered the home of a Gentile, let alone eaten with one. Up until then, like all observant Jews, Peter had believed 'that it is against our law for a Jew to associate with a Gentile or visit him' (Acts 10:28), and so far nothing in his Christian experience had led him to question this. So overwhelming was the leading of the Holy Spirit that

Peter shattered two life-long taboos in one day.

There was trouble back in Jerusalem. 'The circumcised believers criticised him and said, "You went into the house of uncircumcised men and ate with them"' (Acts 11:2f.). When Peter patiently explained how the Holy Spirit had led him at every amazing step, his critics had to agree, 'So then, God has granted even the Gentiles repentance unto life' (Acts 11:18). But questions still remained. For the basic position was quite clear, and always had been: if Gentiles wanted to enjoy the blessings of the covenant for themselves, they could do so – but they would have to join the elect people of God by accepting circumcision and committing themselves to the life of obedience to the law of Moses which circumcision symbolized. Until then, there had been no other way.

What conclusion should be drawn from Peter's extra-ordinary experience? Some Jewish Christians concluded that it changed nothing. The Holy Spirit was not changing the rules, simply bypassing them in one instance. They continued to maintain – with increasing fervour – that 'The Gentiles must be circumcised and required to obey the law of Moses', as some of them emphatically put it at the special Council of Jerusalem some time later (Acts 15:5).

The trouble was, the Holy Spirit went on bypassing the rules. Luke now introduces us to what had been happening in the meantime at Antioch in Syria, at this time one of the largest cities in the world and a place of enormous influence. Some of Stephen's friends and supporters, sharing his vision of a world-wide, temple-less knowledge of God through Jesus, had started to proclaim the gospel to the Gentiles in Antioch, and had met with considerable success (Acts 11:19–21). There grew up in Antioch, for the very first time, a church which was not linked to a synagogue, composed of Gentiles and adventurous Jews, who had followed Peter's example and thrown aside the scruples of a lifetime to enter into table-fellowship with their new brethren in Christ. It is not surprising that people felt the need for a new name to describe what was now obviously a new group, and so they hit upon the nickname 'Christians', because Christ was the distinctive possession of all its members, whether Jewish or Gentile (Acts 11:26).

Enter Paul

Paul was a member of this church in Antioch. And he remained a member of it, all through his ministry. It was his spiritual home, the base to which he would return from his missionary journeys, and from which he would again be sent out (Acts 13:1–3; 14:26–28; 15:35f; 18:22f). This close relationship arose out of his commitment to the Antioch vision of church life – of a church from which the law had been banished, and Jews and Gentiles were joined to each other by their common faith in Christ and their common possession of the Holy Spirit. It is not hard to imagine the feelings aroused in Jerusalem by this flagrant disregard of the law. The situation held all the potential for a monumental split. How could Jews and Gentiles learn to live together in one body? The trouble was, somebody would have to compromise. But which side should it be? Should the Jews compromise their commitment to the law, as they had done in Antioch? Or should Gentile Christians overcome their natural antipathy to circumcision and basically adopt a Jewish life-style? This was the favoured option in Jerusalem.

It is worth asking, What had led Paul, who had a Jewish pedigree second to none (*cf.* Phil. 3:4–6), to this extraordinary renunciation of the law? The question is hard to answer. But we must remember the dramatic experience which turned him from persecutor into propagator (Acts 9:1–19), and reflect on the fact that it was zeal for the law which drove him to persecute the church (Gal. 1:13–14). But he then discovered that the law had actually been leading him to persecute the Messiah (Acts 9:5). If, after this, he felt rather negatively about the law, we can hardly be surprised. His conversion meant a radical change of heart towards it.

Paul set out with Barnabas to found other churches on Antiochian principles in Cyprus and southern Turkey (including probably the churches to which he later wrote Galatians). We find the story in Acts 13 – 14. Shortly after they returned, a potential clash with the Jerusalem church was brought much closer by the arrival at Antioch of some Jewish Christians 'from Judea', who laid down a frontal challenge to the Antioch vision of the church by insisting: 'Unless you are circumcised according to the custom taught by Moses, you cannot be saved' (Acts 15:1). Luke's comment is wry, and we can well imagine the scene which ensued: 'This brought Paul and Barnabas into sharp dispute and debate with them' (Acts 15:2). The outcome was the calling of a special Council in Jerusalem, specifically to sort out this disagreement, and Paul and Barnabas were despatched to Jerusalem as the representatives of the Antioch church.

Luke tells the story of the Council in Acts 15:2–29. Its result was a milestone on the way to that fateful decision, twenty years later, which marked the parting of the ways between the church and Judaism. Essentially, it endorsed the rightness of the Antioch theory and practice, although certain concessions were made to Jewish scruples. In the communiqué which was issued afterwards, Gentile believers were asked to compromise, and undertake the minimum legal observances which would make it possible for table fellowship to continue with Jewish Christians of all types (Acts 15:28–29).

Especially interesting is the speech of James which, according to Luke, brought the Council to its decision (Acts 15:13–21). James recognized that, in drawing the Gentiles into the blessings of messianic faith, God was simply fulfilling Old Testament prophecy. So, while in one sense the law was being violated by their inclusion without circumcision, in another sense the Old Testament was being fulfilled.

It was left to Paul to tackle the problem posed by this dual approach to the Old Testament. Galatians and Romans both deal with it, and with the accompanying issues concerning the law, the covenant with Israel, and the blessing of the Gentiles. This is the theological setting of Romans 9 – 11, which represents the summit of the mountain, the peak of Paul's achievement in reconciling his law-free gospel with continued acceptance of the Old Testament. In fact both Galatians and Romans can be seen as his defence of the Antioch understanding of the church against its opponents – or as his explanation of the action of the Holy Spirit in blessing the Gentiles without reference to the Old Testament law and Israel's covenant position.

It is worthwhile considering the background to Romans in greater detail, so that we may be as clear as possible about the issues at stake.

Trouble in Galatia

Reading between the lines, it seems likely that, while Paul was travelling to Jerusalem for the Council, representatives of the hard-line 'circumcision party' were heading in the opposite direction, towards the churches which he and Barnabas had founded on their first missionary journey together, with the intention of putting right the damage they thought Paul had done. The letter to the Galatians was probably written not long after the Council, prompted by the fact that some of the Gentile Christians in Galatia had been yielding to pressure to be circumcised. Paul's passionate letter reveals just how strongly he felt about this. For him, accepting circumcision was tantamount to being cut off from Christ (Gal. 5:4). 'I am astonished that you are so quickly deserting the one who called you by the grace of Christ and are turning to a different gospel!' he cries (Gal. 1:6).

Galatians records a painful public clash between Paul and Peter over the issue (Gal. 2:11ff.). Peter had come to Antioch, perhaps in order to help communicate the Council's decision. At first, he followed the new way he had learned in Cornelius' house, and joined in fellowship with the Gentile believers. But then he separated himself, under pressure from the 'circumcision group' (Gal. 2:12). Perhaps they pointed out to him that the Gentile believers in Antioch seemed unwilling to adopt the minimum legal requirements laid on them by the Council, and suggested that they ought to be given a vivid lesson of the consequences of continuing to be uncooperative.

Whatever the reasons, Peter withdrew from table-fellowship in Antioch, which meant, of course, no longer sharing the Lord's Supper with fellow Gentile believers. Paul felt that the whole gospel was at stake. 'I opposed him to his face, because he was clearly in the wrong . . . they were not acting in line with the truth of the gospel' (Gal. 2:11, 14). By explaining his reasons for this dramatic head-on clash with Peter, Paul hoped to get across to the Galatians the reasons why they too should not submit to being pushed in the same direction, into Judaism. Galatians 2:16 puts it in a nutshell: '[We] know that a man is not justified by observing the law, but by faith in Jesus Christ.'

For Paul, there was no question of seeking an acceptable compromise between the two sides. The Jews cannot insist that Gentiles adopt the law, because it has been excluded from the salvation brought by the Messiah, and all men, Jews and Gentiles alike, are now to be 'justified' solely by faith. Galatians is devoted to arguing the truth of this position.

Trouble in Jerusalem

Sadly, we do not know what effect Galatians had on its recipients. It cannot have enhanced Paul's reputation in Jerusalem. When he actually travelled there some years later, James welcomed him and rejoiced over the successes of his ministry among the Gentiles, but then warned him that the 'thousands' of Jewish converts in Jerusalem were all 'zealous for the law' (Acts 21:20). He continued,

> *They have been informed that you teach all the Jews who live among the Gentiles to turn away from Moses, telling them not to circumcise their children or live according to our customs.* (Acts 21:21)

James was anxious to do something to show that 'there is no truth in these reports about you' (Acts 21:24). But, of course, there *was* truth in them. They were exaggerated – it was legal observance by *Gentiles* which Paul strongly opposed. He did not directly tell Christian Jews to 'turn away from Moses', but he himself had given up legal observances in order better to evangelize the Gentiles (1 Cor. 9;21), and insisted that such practices were matters of complete indifference as far as Christian discipleship was concerned (1 Cor. 7:19; Gal. 5:6; Rom. 14:1–8). There can be no doubt about it: if some of the Jerusalem Christians, 'zealous for the law', had got hold of a copy of Galatians (which is not at all unlikely), they would have been horrified by what they read:

*Mark my words! I, Paul, tell you that if you let yourselves
be circumcised, Christ will be of no value to you at all. . . .
You who are trying to be justified by law have been alienated
from Christ; you have fallen away from grace . . .* (Gal.
5:2, 4)

Although this is a warning to Gentiles tempted to accept
circumcision, such verses could easily have been read as an
attack on Jewish Christianity as such.

Trouble in Rome

Romans was written when Paul was preparing for the visit to
Jerusalem mentioned above (Rom. 15:25). He was obviously
apprehensive about what he might encounter there (Rom.
15:31). Perhaps we can gain some insight into the purpose
behind Romans as we reflect on Paul's tricky situation at this
time. For it has often puzzled scholars why he should devote
such effort to writing such a mammoth letter to a church he
had never visited – a letter which amounts to a rounded
defence of his whole gospel. It has also puzzled scholars how
Paul seems to know so many people in the Roman church,
never having been there. Twenty-six people are greeted by
name in Romans 16:3–15, and many others by association –
far more than in any other letter.

The answer to both puzzles appears when we remember
what sort of a place Rome was. It was the centre of the world.
There was constant traffic between Rome and the rest of the
empire. This fact alone explains how Paul knew so many
people there. But also, there was constant interchange
between Jerusalem and the huge Jewish population in Rome,
and Paul knew well that disparaging views of his ministry
would long since have travelled to Rome. In fact he had his
own spies there: Priscilla and Aquila (Rom. 16:3) were old
friends who had supported his ministry in Corinth and
Ephesus, and they would have told him the situation.

Precisely because Rome was the hub of the universe, Paul
wanted to get the church there on his side. It appears from
Romans 15:18–24, 28f. that he wanted to move his sphere of

operations into the western half of the Mediterranean, and obviously he would no longer be able to have Antioch as his base. Rome would make an excellent substitute. But the church there would need to be wholly behind his gospel, which at the moment it seems, it was not. Hence the letter to the Romans – which tackles as its central concern all these basic questions about the relationship between the church and Israel.

As we read the letter carefully, we can gather some of the accusations which were being made against Paul and his gospel, and sense the tense relationship between Jewish and Gentile Christians in the Roman church. In particular, we discover from chapters 14 – 15 that the church was divided over the issues of food and of festivals (14:2–6). The same old trouble reappears. Paul insists that Jews and Gentiles must simply live together, accepting one another 'just as Christ accepted you' (15:7), not judging one another or denying each his conscientious convictions before God (14:4f., 10, 13). However, Paul knew well that this kind of disagreement could not be solved by a dose of warm-heartedness. Behind it lay theological disagreement about the covenant and the people of God, which would have to be sorted out if harmony were to prevail. Hence the rest of Romans.

The structure of Romans

Romans 3:1–8 raises the basic issues which set the scene for the whole letter. Here Paul lists a string of objections or accusations which had been made against him.

1. He was charged with denying Israel the privilege of being the recipient of God's covenant (v. 1). Paul rejects this charge (v. 2).

2. He was charged with making Israel's rejection of Christ far more significant than it really is, suggesting that her faithlessness will make God faithless too (v. 3). No, says Paul – of course God will remain faithful to his covenant (v. 4).

3. He was accused of throwing the law out of the window as part of his gospel message, turning black into white, seeking to prove God's righteousness by his approval of law-lessness

(v. 5). No, Paul replies: I am not undermining morality by my doctrine of justification apart from the law (v. 6).

4. Yes, you are! comes the imagined reply. Because you cast the law aside, you are in effect saying, 'Let us do evil that good may come' (vv. 7–8a). No, Paul says: it is you who are in danger of condemnation.

Paul simply lists and rejects these charges here. In fact they boil down to two distinct but inter-linked issues, and he treats them as such, dealing with one in Romans 3 – 8 and the other in 9 – 11. They are really the two sides of one coin, and so these two sections are closely related to each other.

Romans 3 – 8 picks up objections 3 and 4 above (Rom. 3:5–8). It is a little difficult for Gentile readers to enter into the distinctive Jewish understanding of the law which underlies this argument. For the Jew, the law was the supremely wonderful possession bestowed by God on his people, the concrete expression of his love for Israel. It was not a ladder whereby man could climb up to God; it was a way of life in written form, laid upon his people by the God of Israel, who called them to go that way in obedience to him and in dependence upon his grace. To sum it up in one word: it was righteousness, and Israel was distinguished from the Gentiles by knowing the way of righteousness and by being given grace to walk in it. In fact (and this is something which New Testament scholars have only recently realized with new conviction), Jews generally thought about the law in much the same way as Christians do about the life of discipleship laid upon us – a privilege, a delight, an all-consuming passion, a calling to complete dependence upon God and his grace.

Hence the puzzlement and anger which greeted Paul's rejection of the law. Was he not undermining all righteousness? In answer to this charge, Paul unfolds his doctrine of justification by faith in Romans 3 – 8. We shall have to look back at his argument at several important places as we consider Romans 9 – 11, simply because it is the other side of the same coin, and his thought runs along parallel lines in the two sections. Throughout chapters 3 – 8, he insists that the law must not be allowed to usurp the place which is Christ's alone. He is the 'righteousness from God, apart from law' (3:21), and only those joined to him will be released from the rule of sin so as to become 'slaves to righteousness' (5:21; 6:18). But this does not mean the total rejection of the law. On the contrary, in Christ the law is upheld (3:31), its weakness remedied (8:3–4). As the law takes second place to Christ, righteousness is established, not compromised.

Then, in chapters 9 – 11, he turns the coin over and deals with the other side – objections 1 and 2 above (3:1–4), which amount to the charge that, along with the law, he is throwing aside the whole old covenant, with its promises and the chosen people at its heart. With these chapters, Romans reaches its climax, because 9 – 11 builds upon 3 – 8 as all these themes interweave to produce a compelling vindication of Paul's gospel within the context of the whole biblical revelation.

This chapter has tried to show that the issues and problems which Paul tackles in Romans 9 – 11 are identical with those we face today when we ask, Are the Jews still the chosen people of God? He too was vitally concerned to know whether the old covenant was still valid, and if so, in what sense. He too wrestled with the problem of the relationship between Jews and Gentiles in one church, and with the agonizing fact of Jewish unbelief towards Christ. Like us, he wanted to look into the future, to know whether and in what sense the Old Testament prophecies of the restoration of Israel to her God might be fulfilled. We could hardly ask for a more direct treatment of the questions that concern us. Far from containing a few incidental statements of relevance to the problem of Israel, the whole thrust and sweep of the argument is concerned with it. That is why it is necessary to study all three chapters section by section, rather than just pick out the verses which seem important. Paul's argument is cumulative, and only by seeing how he builds it up can we hear his authentic voice. This is what we will now seek to do.

CHAPTER THREE

Paul weeps over Israel

¹I speak the truth in Christ – I am not lying, my conscience confirms it in the Holy Spirit – ²I have great sorrow and unceasing anguish in my heart. ³For I could wish that I myself were cursed and cut off from Christ for the sake of my brothers, those of my own race, ⁴the people of Israel. Theirs is the adoption as sons; theirs the divine glory, the covenants, the receiving of the law, the temple worship and the promises. ⁵Theirs are the patriarchs, and from them is traced the human ancestry of Christ, who is God over all, for ever praised! Amen. (Romans 9:1–5)

I well remember the deep impression it made on me. 'Read Romans 8 verses 38 and 39,' said the leader of our prayer meeting, looking round at us, a group of eager young Christians with our Bibles open. We did so, in silence. Nothing can separate us from the love of God . . . nothing! The thrill grew within us. 'Now read chapter nine verses one to three' came the voice. Again, we obeyed – and the thrill was replaced by sober thoughtfulness as the penny dropped. Having rejoiced that nothing in all the world could separate him from God's love in Christ, Paul prays that he *may* be separated from it, cut off from Christ for the Jews' sake.

Romans 8:31–39 had long been a favourite 'purple passage' of mine, but I had never before realized how Paul himself responds to the glorious truths he there expresses. He rejoices in his security in Christ, but his rejoicing lives alongside a deep sadness. In fact, the sadness seems to eclipse the joy.

31

This is so unexpected that he has to invoke the names of Christ and the Holy Spirit to prove to his readers that it is true (9:1). And verse 2 is very emphatic: this is no passing sadness, but a 'great sorrow', and an 'unceasing anguish', one which time does not dull nor distractions relieve. In fact the anguish is so great that Paul is prepared to forfeit his wonderful security in Christ, if by this means he could solve the problem. He follows in the footsteps of Moses, who likewise prayed that God would blot his name out of the book of life rather than punish Israel for her sin (Ex. 32:32). It is hard to overestimate the shocking quality of Romans 9:1–3.

Here is the first lesson to draw for ourselves today. Do we, the Christian church, feel the same sort of pain over the unbelief of the Jews? Paul did not feel this way for purely psychological reasons, simply because he happened to be a Jew by birth. He appeals to far more than merely his own background and descent here. In verses 4–5, he sets out the solid theological reasons for feeling the way he did. Really, we must confess that we have not shared his grief. Ever since the church and Judaism parted company nineteen centuries ago, we have not only regarded them as equivalent to the adherents of any other non-Christian religion, but in many times and places have actually persecuted them for not being Christian. This is to our everlasting shame before God. Whatever our conclusions about the overall meaning of Romans 9 – 11 may be, this much is clear: if we are seeking to be New Testament Christians, then we must also seek to share Paul's heart-rending anguish over the unbelief of the Jews.

Israel . . . cut off!

For the problem has not changed. Paul grieved because the vast majority of his Jewish compatriots had failed to respond to the good news of Jesus Christ, and some of them had even become the gospel's fiercest opponents. In city after city he had experienced their opposition to his own ministry (see, for example, Acts 14:2, 19; 17:5, 13; 1 Thes. 2:15–16). How they must have reminded him of his own persecution of the church before his conversion! Looking back, he now understands the

state in which he lived and in which they still are – 'cursed
. . . cut off from Christ!' (v. 3) – and he wishes with all his
heart that he might be able to change places with them.

But that is impossible. For the gospel tells us how God's
own Son has already changed places with us, as Paul explains
in 2 Corinthians 5:21: 'God made him who had no sin to be
sin for us, so that in him we might become the righteousness
of God' (see also Rom. 8:3–4). He takes our sins, and we take
his righteousness, in what must be the most inequitable deal
ever dreamed up. So if Paul's 'brothers', his fellow-Jews, have
turned that deal down, no amount of further offering on Paul's
part will make any difference. All he can do is express his
willingness: 'I could wish . . .'.

Strangely, this deep sense of personal anguish is most
notably absent from the writings of some of the advocates of
the 'Israel theology', as we have dubbed it. We might have
expected them, of all Christians, to have shared Paul's longing
to see the Jews come to faith in Christ. But in many cases the
emphasis falls on appreciating what Israel already is, without
Christ. We are not told that, because of their special position
in God's purposes, the gospel must go 'to the Jew first', which
is what Paul teaches (Rom. 1:16). Rather, we are simply told
that we must stand by Israel, recognizing that God still
regards her as his people, and so doing the same ourselves.
Let us be clear from the outset: any Israel theology which
does not start from a deep grief at the Jews' unbelief, and
proceed to an intense longing that they should turn to their
Messiah, cannot claim to be Pauline.

Theological distress

But it is not just a personal tragedy. It is also a theological
problem. Verses 4 and 5 spell this out. Paul takes us on a
tour through the books of Moses, listing all the wonderful
privileges and blessings which God had showered upon his
chosen people. First, he calls them 'the people of Israel' (v.
4) for the first time in Romans, reminding us of the origin of
the nation in the blessing of that undeserving trickster Jacob,
who was transformed and renamed 'Israel' (Gn. 32:28). Then

we move on to the exodus, remembering God's declaration to Pharaoh that Israel was 'my first-born son' (Ex. 4:22), and that he would therefore act to secure his son's release from slavery. 'The divine glory' reminds us of all the manifestations of God's glory to Israel, especially the fiery pillar that led them out of Egypt and the cloud that stood on Mount Sinai and later descended on to the tabernacle (Ex. 13:21; 19:16; 40:34). 'The covenants' expresses the commitment of the Lord which underlay his action to save Israel, his determination to be Israel's God for ever. The original covenant with Abraham (Gn. 17:7) was later renewed with Israel (Ex. 19:6; *etc.*) and then focused specially upon David (2 Sa. 7:16).

'The receiving of the law' happened next. The gift of the law was and still is felt to be the most signal mark of God's blessing and love for Israel. 'The temple worship' followed on, focusing that obedience and blessing in one particular place, first the tabernacle and later the temple, where God's glory dwelt and man was invited to come before him with repentance and sacrifice. And finally 'the promises' and 'the patriarchs' sum it all up: God will not, cannot, go back on his word to save his people and to be their God. Abraham, Isaac and Jacob (the patriarchs) received those promises and then experienced for themselves what God has promised to all their descendants, as they were upheld and protected by him through many trials and tribulations.

This list is a beautiful example of the careful thought and construction that underlies all Paul's writing. Not only do its six items follow on from each other, tracing the early history of God's people, but they also balance each other in two different ways. They naturally fall into two groups of three: items 1–3 focus on the privileges which God gave to Israel, his unreserved acts of grace. Items 4–6 then also suggest the consequent responsibilities resting on Israel, especially obedience to the law and the true worship of the Lord.

But within this balance they also form pairs. The first ('adoption') and the fourth ('the receiving of the law') go together (in fact the Greek words rhyme with each other – *hyiothesia, nomothesia*), and so do the second and the fifth, and the third and the sixth. The first pair reminds us pointedly how the glorious privilege of being God's children is matched by the responsibility of obeying the family rules (see for instance Dt. 32:5–6). The second pair, 'glory' and 'worship', go together because God's glory, the 'Shekinah', rested upon Israel's places of worship (the tabernacle and the temple) as a permanent reminder of the holiness demanded of his people, if he were to dwell in their midst. Thirdly, 'covenants' and 'promises' go together throughout the Bible (see for instance Eph. 2:12), because God's promises were issued on the strength of the covenant relationship between him and his people. Deuteronomy 28 expresses this clearly: because they are his people, God promises both 'blessings' and 'curses', depending on their response.

But the deepest theological distress arises from the fact that Paul does not just have the Old Testament in mind here. He has used several of these expressions earlier in Romans, applying them specifically to Christians. As believers, we have received 'the Spirit of adoption' (8:15), and long for the day when the final court order is made, finalizing our admittance into God's family (8:23). We rejoice in our hope of God's glory (5:2), and realize that in Christ we have already been glorified (8:30); and we too look back to Abraham as our father (4:11–12), for he is father of all who are justified by faith in Christ.

So when Paul says in 9:4 'Theirs is . . .', he does not just mean that these are the blessings showered upon Israel in the Old Testament. He also means that Israel should possess their New Testament counterparts, so wonderfully described in the preceding chapters. She is the rightful possessor of all that Christ has done for us. This is a vital thought in the whole argument of Romans 9 – 11. Paul puts it in a nutshell in 15:27, where he writes simply of Gentile Christians sharing 'in the Jews' spiritual blessings'. They have failed to enter into their rightful inheritance. This is why Paul feels such anguish, for, whatever his opponents may say, he does not throw the Old Testament away, and he knows how the blessings of the New Testament grow out of the Old.

A Gentile take-over?

But the problem was not just that Israel had failed to enter
the door of blessing opened for her by Jesus. It looked as
though God had changed his mind. Gentiles were flooding
into the church through the missionary activity of Paul and
others, being filled with the Spirit and baptized entirely
without reference to Israel and the Old Testament. Paul did
his best to teach the Old Testament to his Gentile converts,
but – as we have seen – he certainly did not require them to
be circumcised, which was the sign of entry into God's people
under Old Testament law, yet in spite of that, the blessing
continued. What conclusion were people to draw from this
outpouring of the Holy Spirit on the Gentiles? Not surprisingly, some Gentile believers concluded that God had finished
with Israel, because of her final rejection of the Messiah, and
argued that the church had now replaced Israel as the chosen
people of the new covenant.

This, of course, is precisely what the hard-line Jewish
Christians of Jerusalem accused Paul of teaching. But he
could not go that far. He was really in a cleft stick: for, on
the one hand, he wanted to insist that the law had been set
aside as far as salvation was concerned. But, on the other
hand, he saw clearly that if God had gone back on the Old
Testament, he could go back on the New as well. If Israel
could not trust his promises, how can Christians? As we have
seen, this is the inner logic which prompts 9:1–5 after 8:31–39.
It looks as though Paul tries to have his cake and eat it.
Wanting to maintain God's faithfulness to his promises, he
was faced with the problem, Why has God allowed Israel to
sink into unbelief? And why is he blessing the Gentiles in this
way? But wanting also to banish the law from salvation, he
was troubled by the thought, Isn't Israel's failure and the
Gentiles' inclusion just what we would expect – if God has
set his law aside?

The greatest tragedy of all?

Paul's final thought in this opening paragraph is the final

twist of the knife in his heart. Jesus, the Christ, the centre of all God's purposes for the world, was born of the stock of Israel (v. 5). Paul magnifies the greatness of this privilege by taking the step of actually calling Christ 'God'. Some translations have punctuated the sentence differently, in order to avoid applying this highest of all titles to Christ – and it is certainly something which Paul does very sparingly. But it is much the most natural way of reading the sentence, however unusual. Perhaps there is a hidden significance in it. It is indeed the greatest tragedy of all, that God himself, incarnate in his Christ, should be rejected by his chosen people – but if Christ really is God . . . can that rejection be the last word? Would God be God if that were so? Perhaps Paul is dropping a hint here. In the long run, can we really believe that the Messiah – who is God! – failed completely in his mission to his people?

The note of praise that springs to Paul's lips is vital. 'God over all, for ever praised!' Whatever the answer to these vexing questions, God-revealed-in-Christ is supremely praiseworthy, and his praise will never cease. That is also the thought which brings Romans 9 – 11 to a close (11:33–36). Whatever the pain or the puzzlement, to praise and worship him is an overriding duty and an untold joy.

CHAPTER FOUR

A nation divided ... by God

> *⁶It is not as though God's word had failed. For not all who are descended from Israel are Israel. ⁷Nor because they are his descendants are they all Abraham's children. On the contrary, 'It is through Isaac that your offspring will be reckoned.' ⁸In other words, it is not the natural children who are God's children, but it is the children of the promise who are regarded as Abraham's offspring. ⁹For this was how the promise was stated: 'At the appointed time I will return, and Sarah will have a son.'*
>
> *¹⁰Not only that, but Rebekah's children had one and the same father, our father Isaac. ¹¹Yet, before the twins were born or had done anything good or bad – in order that God's purpose in election might stand: ¹²not by works but by him who calls – she was told, 'The older will serve the younger.' ¹³Just as it is written: 'Jacob I loved, but Esau I hated.'* (Romans 9:6–13)

Paul in fact writes a 'But' at the beginning of verse 6, for verse 6 is his refusal to draw the apparently unavoidable conclusion from Israel's apostasy and the Gentiles' faith. No, he insists, God's word has not failed. The whole of the rest of Romans 9 – 11 is devoted to proving this assertion. Whatever historical circumstances may seem to say, the truth is otherwise. Looking at it from God's perspective, Paul will boldly argue that the heart-rending fact of Israel's failure is all part of his purpose to keep his word to her.

Right through the Old Testament

It is hardly surprising, therefore, that chapters 9 – 11 are full of Old Testament quotations – some thirty of them, in fact. For Paul must turn to the Old Testament in order to prove this assertion that God's word has not failed. And it is interesting to note that, of the ten quotations which occur in the first main section of his argument, 9:6–29, all but two of them are 'words' actually uttered by the Lord. In order to establish his 'word' to Israel, Paul invites us to go back with him into the Old Testament and hear God speaking all over again, so as to understand what precisely was his promise and commitment to Israel.

We saw in the last chapter how the list of blessings in 9:4–5 takes us on a tour through the five books of Moses. Something similar happens here, for 9:6–29 progresses right through the Old Testament, starting with Abraham (v. 7), and moving on through the other patriarchs (vv. 10, 13) to the exodus (vv. 15, 17), and then on to the prophets (vv. 25, 27). We listen again to God's stated purpose throughout the Old Testament. Paul wants to show that he has dealt consistently with his people throughout their history, and that he has not now changed his mind.

In these particular verses, 9:6–13, Paul lays a foundation which is vital for the whole argument of Romans 9 – 11. It is vital for us, therefore, to be as careful as possible in interpreting him here. Unfortunately, there has been, and still is, much disagreement among theologians about these verses. For not only are there some rather obscure statements, but also many Christians have found it hard to accept what Paul seems to say. It is a considerable challenge, not only to interpret his Greek correctly, but also just to listen to him, and to let him say exactly what he wants to say, even if it seems alien or unacceptable at first sight. That kind of listening is the most vital element in Bible study, sadly lacking sometimes even in learned commentators. The remarkable thing is that, when we have struggled to understand Paul correctly, we often discover that he is not so alien after all, and our views of what we can accept have shifted in his favour. And he helps us along: he has touched on many of these themes earlier in Romans, and we can interpret his meaning here by reference to what he has said before.

Putting it in a nutshell

I believe that we can summarize the message of these verses in the following four points.

1. Not every Jew can claim to belong to 'Israel' just because he can trace his family tree back to Abraham. 'Israel' is a special name full of spiritual significance, and to claim to be a member is to claim to have had a spiritual experience which is not guaranteed just by a birth-certificate. (Paul makes the same point here about 'Israel' as he made in 2:28–29 about the name 'Jew': 'A man is not a Jew if he is only one outwardly, nor is circumcision merely outward and physical. No, a man is a Jew if he is one inwardly; and circumcision is circumcision of the heart, by the Spirit. . .'.)

2. The distinction amongst Jews between those who can rightly claim the name 'Israel' and those who cannot, rests upon the decision or decree of God, who decides, entirely without reference to what we deserve, who shall be 'a child of promise' – that is, a descendant of Abraham to whom the promise 'I will be God to you' is individually applicable.

3. This distinguishing activity of God is no new feature of his dealing with the nation Israel, but goes right back to the beginning, and can be seen in his discriminatory treatment of the children of Abraham and Isaac: he first chose Isaac and not Ishmael, and then Jacob and not Esau.

4. So, tragic though it is, the failure of many Jews to enter into the blessings of the Messiah does not in itself mean that God has abandoned his commitment to Israel.

These four points are the essence of Paul's argument in these verses. It is immediately obvious why some have found it unacceptable. It seems so unfair, that God should distinguish between people in this way. Have we rightly interpreted him? I believe that the correctness of this general interpretation is confirmed by the fact that Paul himself poses this very objection to his own argument in verses 14 and 19, as we shall see.

He can read our minds. If he himself felt that this objection would occur to his readers, we can be fairly sure that he really is saying this, however extraordinary it seems. His argument has two stages in it.

Verses 7–9: discrimination between brothers

Sadly, the NIV could have done better in its translation of verse 7. Paul's Greek is difficult here, but a better translation would be: 'Nor are all Abraham's children also Abraham's seed: on the contrary, "It is through Isaac that your seed will be called." ' The word 'seed' is vital here. It links the quotation, from Genesis 21:12, with the statement it is meant to prove. Paul is using 'seed' with the technical sense which he gave it in Romans 4, where he wrote previously about Abraham's 'seed', defining it collectively as all those who follow in the footsteps of Abraham's faith, whether physically descended from him or not (see 4:16). Following on in 4:17, he radically interprets the promise of Genesis 17:7, 'I will be God to you and to your seed after you', to include Gentiles who believe in God as Abraham did. Here in Romans 9 the Gentiles are not in mind, but the same thought of spiritual (rather than just physical) kinship with Abraham is governing his thinking.

This is the vital point made by this quotation of Genesis 21:12. In the context of the story from which it is taken, its force is, 'In Isaac as opposed to Ishmael will your "seed" be called'. Ishmael was Abraham's much-loved first-born, his son by the slave-girl Hagar whom he took when there seemed to be no fulfilment of the promise of children by his wife Sarah. But he was running ahead of God. God gave him Isaac by Sarah, and now declares that Isaac represents the line of promise, not Ishmael.

Verse 8 then draws the conclusions for contemporary Israel: God is still distinguishing between 'the natural children' (like Ishmael), whose kinship with Abraham is purely physical, and 'the children of promise' (like Isaac), who are related to him not just physically but also spiritually. Abraham did not simply have to produce a son and heir in order to pass on God's glorious promises to his descendants. He had to wait until God pronounced the decree by which alone the 'child of promise' could be born: 'At the appointed time I will return, and Sarah will have a son' (v. 9). Such a decree is still necessary: Paul has already anticipated the rather strange use of the word 'call' in Genesis 21:12 by talking about the way God 'calls' those whom he has predestined to be his (Rom. 8:30). There God's 'call' is the action by which he puts into effect his determination to 'justify' and 'glorify' those whom he has chosen. Paul now applies this principle to contemporary Israel: without a specific 'call' from God, a 'child of the flesh' cannot become a 'child of promise', inheriting for himself or herself the covenant blessings.

Verses 10–13: discrimination between twins

The further example of Jacob and Esau in verses 10–13 simply presses the point home. It could be argued that the promise about Isaac was simply God's adjudication in the dispute about who should be Abraham's heir. After all, he had two wives, and in cases where a subordinate wife gave birth to the first-born son the law was not at all clear about inheritance. Sarah certainly did her best to ensure that Isaac would face no challenge from Ishmael – and it was her cruel effort to get Hagar and Ishmael thrown out of the family nest which prompted the Lord's pronouncement (Gn. 21:8–14). Can Genesis 21:12 really bear the full weight that Paul rests upon it? He seems to be aware of this problem, for in the case of Jacob and Esau:

1. there was absolutely no distinction of origin (v. 10);

2. there was absolutely no distinction of achievement or moral character (v. 11);

3. and yet there was a clear distinction of destiny, as attested by Genesis 25:23 (v. 12).

The only possible basis upon which this distinction could

have been made, argues Paul, was 'God's purpose in election' (v. 11), because no identifiable human factors separate two babies in one womb. And that (he suggests, by implication) is precisely what is going on in the Israel over which he grieves. Her apostasy does not in itself mean that God has terminated his dealings with her. He exercises his prerogative of 'election' still: choosing one and not another, 'calling' those he chooses to himself (v. 12). We remember another use of the word 'call' earlier in Romans, in 4:17: 'God . . . brings the dead to life and calls into being what does not exist' (Jerusalem Bible). There, Paul was referring to the miracle of Isaac's birth when both his parents were 'as good as dead' (4:19), well past child-bearing age. In that situation, God's 'call' went out, and Isaac was born. Now, Paul finds another act of 'calling' in the next generation, when the Creator again steps in to declare that Jacob, not Esau, is to be the father of the nation through which all nations will be blessed (see Genesis 28:13–14).

Can it be true?

Looking through these verses more slowly in this way just seems to make the problem worse. How can it be fair to treat people in this way? But behind this question lies an even more serious one: What good does it do, anyway, to be a Jew? Paul seems to be saying that, for all the apparent sureness of his wonderful promises to Israel, God reserves the right to withdraw them whenever he wants. Can that be true? As we have already seen, when Paul faced the question in 3:1, 'What advantage is there in being a Jew?', his reply was, 'Much in every way!' (3:2). But how can he really say that? These are precisely the objections which he considers in the very next section, 9:14–18, and he will bear them in mind throughout these three chapters.

But the quotation of Malachi 1:2–3 in verse 13 gives us a little hint of the direction in which Paul's argument is going to move. For Malachi uses the names 'Jacob' and 'Esau' to refer not just to these two individuals, but also to the two nations descended from them (Israel and Edom). Somehow the character or quality of the choice made by God between Jacob and Esau is transferred to the descendants of each. By his quotation of Malachi, Paul endorses a *corporate* understanding of election. The discriminating 'calling' in verses 7–12 does not mean that God abandons his commitment to the nation Israel as such. When he 'loved' Jacob, the Lord pledged his love also to all Jacob's descendants. But how can Paul hold all this together? At one moment he seems to say that Jews cannot rely on their membership of the nation Israel for enjoyment of God's promises, and then a moment later implies that God committed himself to Israel through the promises made to the patriarchs. We would be in the company of some eminent scholars if we were to say to him, 'Paul, you can't have it both ways!'

I believe that Paul is well aware of this, and that he will produce a satisfying answer to this problem. For the moment, let us simply ask him, In what sense did the Lord 'hate' Esau? Did he hate him and his descendants, the Gentile Edomites, in such a way that both he and they would remain for ever outside the orbit of his grace and his 'call'? Paul cannot understand Malachi 1:2–3 in this way, for then he would be pulling the carpet out from underneath his entire ministry to the Gentiles. What right would he have to evangelize the Gentiles, including the Edomites, if God had decreed their eternal exclusion? He is moving towards saying that the covenant of God with Israel neither guarantees permanent inclusion for Israel nor permanent exclusion for the Gentiles, but is a signal of his commitment to save the whole world . . . but we must not anticipate him.

Additional note

It is hardly surprising that scholars have tried to find alternative interpretations of Paul's teaching here. Basically, two alternatives are offered:

The 'groups, not individuals' interpretation

According to this first view, Paul does not think of God distinguishing between individuals – rather, between nations. The 'clue' for this is found in the observation which we have already made about the quotation of Malachi 1:2–3 in verse 13, that 'Jacob' and 'Esau' stand for Israel and Edom. So, scholars argue, the same must be true for Abraham and Isaac (and Ishmael): in each case God is separating nations, making one rather than another the recipient of his promises and grace. In this way, the sting is taken out of an interpretation which seems to imply a harsh and arbitrary discrimination between individuals. This sometimes goes hand-in-hand with the second alternative:

The 'service, not salvation' interpretation

According to this, Paul is concerned entirely with the destiny of individuals or nations within their lives or within world history, and not with their destiny in eternity: he does not teach that people's eternal salvation depends upon God's election of them (or not), but rather that God chooses what part they will play in the world, and whether they will mediate his grace to the world or not. The 'clue' for this interpretation is found in the treatment of Pharaoh in verse 17, where 'raised you up for this very purpose' could simply mean, 'gave you this particular role to play in the drama of human history'. Pharaoh was raised on to the stage of world history in order to provide a wonderful demonstration of God's power – so his own personal standing before God is not in view at all. Then the idea is read back into 9:6–13: likewise Abraham, Isaac and Jacob (or the nation they represent) have been chosen by God to be the vehicle of his grace in the world, elected to service rather than to salvation.

Weighing them up

Attractive though they are in some respects, I do not think that either of these viewpoints does justice to Paul's language in 9:6–13, nor to the overall thrust of his argument.

1. Paul's Jewish-Christian readers would feel that all their suspicions about his attitude to the law and the Old Testament had been confirmed, if they heard him say that God's election of the patriarchs was not 'unto salvation'. What a devaluing of the Old Testament! If this really is what Paul

teaches in these verses, it sits very uneasily alongside the list of privileges in 9:4–5. And indeed, Paul has already said that Abraham was 'justified by faith' in God's promises, just as we now are through faith in Christ (Rom. 4, especially vv. 1–3, 9–12, 19–25). In line with this, Paul uses in 9:6–13 all sorts of terms which he has previously used in connection with salvation in and through Christ: 'seed' (*cf.* 4:11–13), 'God's children' (*cf.* 8:15–17), 'God's purpose' (*cf.* 8:28), 'call' (*cf.* 8:28, 30), 'election' (*cf.* 8:33), and even the innocent-looking word 'regarded' in verse 8, to which great spiritual force is attached in 4:6–11, 22–24 (where it is translated 'credit' or 'count' by NIV). Having used all these expressions in connection with salvation, in some cases only a few verses earlier in Romans, it would be impossible for Paul to have anything else in mind in Romans 9. In any case, it is the possibility of Israel falling out of salvation which worries him so much.

2. The only time when Paul actually mentions 'service' in these verses, it is the other way round: in verse 12 it is Esau who serves Jacob, not vice versa. In any case, how do Ishmael and Esau fit into the picture in the 'service, not salvation' interpretation? The patriarchs and Israel clearly have a 'role' in history – to be the vehicle of God's grace, the prophet of his love to the world. But what corresponding role could Esau have? The trouble is that this interpretation depends on reading an idea back from verse 17 into this earlier passage. In verse 17, Paul certainly has in mind some such notion of the 'role' that God made Pharaoh play in the drama of the exodus. But it is not at all clear that he thus gives us the 'clue' to the interpretation of the whole passage. In any case, this distinction between 'service' and 'salvation' is not helpful, for it is precisely through our response of faith and obedience (or of unbelief and disobedience) in this life that our eternal destiny is forged (see Rom. 2:5–11). Pharaoh's actions were by no means indifferent, as far as his eternal destiny was concerned.

3. Paul is certainly concerned with groups and nations in Romans 9 – 11; after all, the problem is all about the relationship between Jews and Gentiles in God's purposes. But just

at this point, it would be no help at all to say that God has chosen Israel out of all the Gentile nations – for that is precisely the problem. Neither Paul nor his opponents disputed God's election of Israel. The argument was over whether God had turned from her and abandoned his promise. Just to restate the fact of Israel's election would contribute nothing to the solution of the agonizing problem that Paul is tackling.

4. These interpretations seem to be motivated, not by openness to the text, but by a desire not to let Paul say what is indeed an uncomfortable thing to hear – that God elects some individuals to salvation, and not others. One commentator fulminates, 'We should cease to exploit these texts to maintain a doctrine . . . that . . . is not only of frightful cruelty but also exegetically untenable.'[1] Leenhardt makes it clear where his priority lies. Exegesis is the 'but also' which follows the really determining consideration – a judgment about the 'cruelty' of Paul's teaching. But exegesis is the first and most vital task: having understood the text, we then accommodate ourselves to what we have found. And is this interpretation really 'exegetically untenable'? Reading verses 6–8, it is surely impossible to maintain anything else. The name 'Israel' is only rightfully borne by the 'children of promise' within the nation, who by God's 'purpose in election' have been made his children, with all that that implies of regeneration and the indwelling of his Spirit (8:9–17), and it is they who have entered into the fulfilment of all the glorious privileges and promises given to Israel in the Old Testament. Hence the apostasy of so many Jews does not of itself imply God's abandonment of Israel.

Yes, but . . .

Yet we surely share Leenhardt's instinctive feeling. How can this be just or fair? It is like promising to take the whole of Class 4A camping by the sea, and then moving half the children into 4B the day before the holiday. Paul enters this minefield in the next section – uncompromisingly.

---

[1] F. J. Leenhardt, *The Epistle to the Romans* (Lutterworth, 1961), p. 250.

CHAPTER FIVE

Has God treated Israel fairly? Yes!

¹⁴What then shall we say? Is God unjust? Not at all! ¹⁵For he says to Moses,

> *'I will have mercy on whom I have mercy,*
> *and I will have compassion on whom I have*
> *compassion.'*

¹⁶It does not, therefore, depend on man's desire or effort, but on God's mercy. ¹⁷For the Scripture says to Pharaoh: 'I raised you up for this very purpose, that I might display my power in you and that my name might be proclaimed in all the earth.' ¹⁸Therefore God has mercy on whom he wants to have mercy, and he hardens whom he wants to harden. (Romans 9:14–18)

Paul is nothing if not courageous. He has just put forward what Professor J. C. O'Neill calls 'a thoroughly immoral doctrine' – and indeed every sensitive person instinctively reacts against the thought that God acts so arbitrarily in his dealings with human beings, consigning us to heaven or hell just as the mood takes him. The great John Wesley, founder of Methodism, preached a famous sermon against predestination precisely on these grounds. But that seems to be what Paul has just taught!

He tackles the charge of injustice head-on. 'Is God unjust? Not at all!' (v. 14). Then he seeks to substantiate his denial, building his argument around two quotations from Exodus, in verses 15 and 17. Here his boldness appears again, for he goes straight to the episode in Exodus about the hardening of Pharaoh's heart, which has likewise caused problems for sensitive souls. It would be all right if Exodus told us simply that Pharaoh, king of Egypt, hardened his own heart in resistance to God's demand to 'let my people go'. But on no fewer than ten occasions we read that God hardened his heart for him (*e.g.* Ex. 9:12; 10:1). It seems incredibly unjust that God should issue the demand, make sure that it is refused, and then pass judgment on Pharaoh for refusing it. So the fact that Paul turns to precisely this passage in order to refute the charge of injustice shows that he is thoroughly convinced of his case.

The golden calf

In verse 15 he quotes Exodus 33:19, and once again the context from which he draws the quotation is vital for its correct interpretation. We are in the aftermath of the incident of the golden calf, and Moses has just made the appeal to God which Paul seems to have in mind in Romans 9:3. At the moment of highest blessing and privilege, having arrived at Mount Sinai to receive the law, the Israelites make and worship an idol. Moses appeals on their behalf for forgiveness, and the Lord repents of his determination to abandon Israel altogether (Ex. 32:9–14, 30–34). Moses again appeals, this time to entreat the Lord to continue to be personally present in the midst of his people, as he had been since the exodus:

> *If your Presence does not go with us, do not send us up from here. How will anyone know that you are pleased with me and with your people unless you go with us? What else will distinguish me and your people from all the other people on the face of the earth?* (Ex. 33:15–16)

In response to this appeal, the Lord grants to Moses the wonderful vision of himself described in Exodus 33:19 – 34:7, at the start of which he makes the promise which Paul quotes: 'I will have mercy on whom I will have mercy, and I will have compassion on whom I will have compassion' (Ex. 33:19).

So the first beneficiary of this promise is Moses, received right into God's presence in the most wonderful way. But it is quite clear that he is received as a representative of the whole people, for in fact (such is God's mercy) the dreadful sin of the golden calf becomes an occasion for renewal and reaffirmation of the covenant, rather than its abrogation. See Exodus 34:8–10.

Importantly, however, this renewal of commitment by God does not mean that there will be no judgment for what has happened. God will still act in judgment, but not in the total and immediate way that he first intended. In fact judgment has merely been postponed: 'When the time comes for me to punish, I will punish them for their sin' (Ex. 32:34b). God 'does not leave the guilty unpunished' (Ex. 34:7), but because he is also merciful, the judgment does not happen straightaway, and he continues to be present with Israel, in spite of her rebellion.

Undeserved mercy

This verse fits Paul's purpose in two ways. Firstly, the situation is identical. Israel is again in a state of awful apostasy, but the golden calf story suggests grounds for solid hope that God will not abandon his commitment to her, however dreadful her unbelief.

Secondly – and more precisely germane to Paul's purpose – Exodus 33:19 shows how mercy is always undeserved. In a situation of universally deserved condemnation, mercy is certainly 'unjust', but who in their right minds would complain about 'injustice' of that sort? The bottom line is clear: to demand justice is to demand that no mercy be shown at all. This is Paul's first answer to the accusation in verse 14: if it is true that God is distinguishing within Israel between 'children of the promise' and 'children of the flesh' (9:8), saving the former but not the latter, then we must remember that the injustice lies, not in making the distinction, but in showing mercy at all. For the constant presupposition of the Bible about mankind is that we deserve nothing but condemnation and death for our rebellion against our Creator. Verse

16 sums it up: 'It does not, therefore, depend on man's desire or effort, but on God's mercy' – for we can do absolutely nothing to earn our way into God's presence. All we can do is delight in the mercy of a King who sends out his servants to sweep us in off the streets into the marriage-feast of his Son, as entirely undeserving guests (Mt. 22:8–10).

Pharaoh's hard heart

In verses 17–18 Paul moves back in time, from the period immediately after the exodus to that immediately preceding it. But why? The commentators scratch their heads over the sudden introduction of Pharaoh into the argument. The first step on the way into Paul's meaning is to notice the balanced way he has composed these verses:

Verse 14: Basic assertion, 'No injustice!'
Verse 15: 'For . . .', followed by scriptural quotation
Verse 16: 'Therefore . . .' (the Greek is emphatic)
Verse 17: 'For . . .', followed by scriptural quotation
Verse 18: 'Therefore . . .' (the same emphatic Greek).

Noticing this balance, some scholars have concluded that Pharaoh is there to provide the opposite side of the picture from Moses. If there is to be selective mercy – and that is the conclusion we draw from the story of the golden calf – then it must follow that there is to be 'hardening' as well. For if God acts in judgment, it must be upon those who, like Pharaoh, have not repented, and who still do not have their hearts set upon him in spite of all they know of him. In spite of all God's appeals to him, and in spite of all the demonstrations of his power in the plagues and the signs which Moses was enabled to perform (Ex. 4:1–9), Pharaoh remained stubbornly resistant to God, 'hardened' in disobedience.

Certainly verse 18 seems to suggest that, for Paul, 'mercy' and 'hardening' are equal and opposite activities of God. However much Pharaoh may have deserved the judgment which eventually fell upon him and his subjects, Paul believed (or so it seems, at first sight) that it was ultimately God's decision to harden him, because he could have 'softened' him if he had wanted to, and shown him mercy, but that was simply not his will.

The trouble with this interpretation – quite apart from the moral problem posed by God directly stiffening people's rebellion against himself – is the 'for' at the beginning of verse 17. If it were 'but', there would be little alternative to interpreting these verses in this way: Moses illustrates mercy, *but* Pharaoh displays hardening – equally at God's hands. But the 'for' suggests that Exodus 9:16 (which Paul quotes in verse 17) is intended to provide further support for verse 16: in other words, Paul is turning to a second text from Exodus in order to amplify and clarify his answer to the charge of injustice. (In any case, if Paul were simply using Pharaoh as an instance of 'hardening', he would have done better to choose one of the many verses in which Pharaoh's rebellion is underlined, like Exodus 5:2, where he says, 'Who is the Lord, that I should obey him and let Israel go? I do not know the Lord . . .'.)

Putting off the evil day

When we look more closely, we discover that Paul is saying something much more subtle. Again the context surrounding his quotation is vital, particularly the preceding verse:

> *For by now I could have stretched out my hand and struck you and your people with a plague that would have wiped you off the earth. But I have raised you up for this very purpose, that I might show you my power and that my name might be proclaimed in all the earth.* (Ex. 9:15f.)

What immediately strikes us is that the idea of the postponement of judgment appears here, just as in the story of the golden calf. Complete destruction is deserved, but God has not carried out such an awful judgment. Instead, he has 'raised Pharaoh up' (this phrase could be translated 'preserved you alive') with the object of demonstrating his power and spreading his name. We naturally ask, Power to do what? and, Name for being what? The answer lies close at hand when we consider the Exodus stories and the way they are treated elsewhere in the Bible: his 'power' is his power to save Israel and make her his people, and his 'name' is his name for being a God who shows mercy and draws people to himself. This was the basis of the appeal that Moses made against the Lord's intended destruction of Israel after the making of the golden calf:

> *Why should your anger burn against your people, whom you brought out of Egypt with great power and a mighty hand? Why should the Egyptians say, 'It was with evil intent that he brought them out . . . to wipe them off the face of the earth'?* (Ex. 32:11f.)

So judgment upon Israel's captors is delayed, because by so doing God can display to them the mercy which motivates his conflict with them. We are strongly reminded of a passage earlier in Romans, which seems designed to prepare the way for this passage here. Getting his sights trained on the man who criticizes others, while committing the same sins himself, Paul cries,

> *Do you show contempt for the riches of his kindness, toler-ance and patience, not realising that God's kindness leads you towards repentance? But because of your stubbornness* [literally, 'hardness'] *and your unrepentant heart, you are storing up wrath against yourself for the day of God's wrath.* (Rom. 2:4f.)

In this passage, Paul is applying to the whole world the same principle of operation by which God acted in Pharaoh's case: he treats us with 'patience' in the face of our 'hardness', appealing for repentance, and delaying the coming of the day of wrath. This is the second element in Paul's reply to the charge of injustice in verse 14. Not only is mercy always undeserved, but judgment is only executed long after it is deserved, and only then (here lies a mystery, to which Paul will return) as part of God's overall plan of salvation. Pharaoh fell under the judgment of God because he was set upon saving Israel, and, through Israel, the whole world.

Paul has still not disposed of the accusation of injustice, however. In the next section he takes his reply further – and he needs to. For one's instinctive response to these two points is to say, 'That's all very well, Paul. But surely, if the basic reason we are still sinners is simply that God has decided not to have mercy on us, how can it be just and right for him to condemn us for our sins?' This is precisely the question he tackles in verse 19.

Additional note

The notion of 'hardening' is a difficult one to grasp. And it is particularly important in Romans 9 – 11, for it reappears in chapter 11, where it plays a crucial role in Paul's whole understanding of the relationship between Jews and Gentiles in the plan of God.

Israel – hardened like Pharaoh?

Verse 18 puts it very starkly. In what sense should we think of God actually 'hardening' Pharaoh in his rebellion against him? – and how does this view of mercy and hardening take Paul further in understanding the apostasy of Israel? We can turn for help both to Exodus and to passages earlier in Romans.

In Exodus, the story of the conflict between the Lord and Egypt begins when Moses is sent back to be the deliverer of Israel. A vital verse is Exodus 3:19, where the Lord says to Moses, in sending him back, 'I know that the king of Egypt will not let you go unless a mighty hand compels him. So I will stretch out my hand and strike the Egyptians . . .' In other words, even before the demand 'Let my people go' is issued, the Lord knows what the response will be, and then as the story proceeds we see that he was quite right (see for example Exodus 7:13), for Pharaoh is quite prepared to maintain his stubbornness in spite of increasingly horrible consequences for himself and his people.

For a theological commentary on this, we can turn to Romans 1:18–32. Here Paul is talking about the rebellion of the whole world, but he might be writing about Pharaoh.

Certainly that gentleman provides a shining example of the refusal to acknowledge the Lord who is revealed clearly in his works (Rom. 1:18–20), of the foolishness of those who worship creature rather than Creator (1:21–23), and supremely of the 'handing-over' process described in 1:24–32, whereby God leaves us to the consequences of our own sin. Three times Paul uses the phrase 'God gave them over' (vv. 24, 26, 28), to pinpoint the pivotal moments in a long process of degeneration, starting with a corruption of true worship (v. 23), and ending with complete depravity of behaviour (vv. 29–32). At each pivotal point, 'God gave them over' does not mean that he is directly instrumental in making them more degenerate than they would otherwise have been. That would be an impossible thought, biblically (see Jas. 1:13–15). Rather, God is declining to step in and deliver them from the natural and inevitable consequences of the sin they have given themselves to. He cannot be blamed if we tear ourselves from him and immerse ourselves ever more deeply in our own darkness, folly and corruption.

That is precisely what 'hardening' is. So when Paul writes, 'God has mercy on whom he wants to have mercy, and he hardens whom he wants to harden' (9:18), he is not describing two equal and opposite activities. 'Mercy' means God stepping in, reversing the trend of our lives towards eternal death by a sovereign act of salvation. But 'hardening' means doing nothing, or rather nothing beyond issuing appeals for repentance which fall on deaf ears, and simply produce an ever greater unwillingness to hear God speak. Romans 2:4–5 sums it up perfectly.

But of course it is still God's decision, to extend mercy or to harden: for if he chooses to go on making appeals which he knows will be rejected, then from one angle he can be regarded as the author of the response, even though no-one is to blame but ourselves, if we turn from him. This is why Exodus can say that God hardened Pharaoh's heart, as well as that Pharaoh hardened his own heart (and was then judged for it). And this is also why Paul turns to Pharaoh in his search for an answer to the problem of Israel's apostasy. There is a deep irony in Paul's argument here, an irony so unexpected and shocking that it is possible to miss the radical nature of what he is saying. His fellow-Jews, because of their rejection of the Messiah, find their spiritual kinship not with the nation freed from slavery, but with the captors who held them in bondage. No wonder his heart was full of 'great sorrow and unceasing anguish' (9:2). Pharaoh lives again, deep in the hearts of the chosen people. Can he be exorcized? Paul agonizes over this in the chapters to come. For if rebellious and unbelieving Pharaoh could be a means of spreading the good news of God's mercy around the world, could there be hope for Israel along the same lines? In the meantime, however, Paul carries forward his rejection of the charge of injustice.

CHAPTER SIX

Is election unjust? No!

> [19]*One of you will say to me: 'Then why does God still blame us? For who resists his will?' [20]But who are you, O man, to talk back to God? 'Shall what is formed say to him who formed it, "Why did you make me like this?"' [21]Does not the potter have the right to make out of the same lump of clay some pottery for noble purposes and some for common use? [22]What if God, choosing to show his wrath and make his power known, bore with great patience the objects of his wrath – prepared for destruction? [23]What if he did this to make the riches of his glory known to the objects of his mercy, whom he prepared in advance for glory – [24]even us, whom he also called, not only from the Jews but also from the Gentiles?* (Romans 9:19–24)

This is one of the most important paragraphs in Romans 9 – 11. It is the climax of this first section (9:6–29), and what Paul writes here is right at the heart of his answer to the problem of Israel. Just for that reason, it is also one of the most difficult sections to interpret. We need to pick our way very carefully through his argument.

Why does God still blame us?

It is hardly surprising that Paul imagines another indignant response from a reader at this point. He does this, in fact, on at least eight occasions in Romans, because he knows he is handling controversial subjects throughout, and deliberately structures his argument around the objections which people had actually put to him in the past. The objection in verse 19 picks up and develops that in verse 14. Paul has done this before, too: there are pairs of objections in Romans 6:1, 15 and 7:7, 13, and in each case the second objection restates the first in the light of the response that Paul has just made to it, so that it becomes even more like a live debate.

In this case, the objection reminds us particularly of the one Paul raises in Romans 3:5 – one he had actually faced, and which seems to underlie the whole argument of Romans. There, it is phrased slightly differently, but it is the same in essence: 'What shall we say? That God is unjust in bringing his wrath on us?' As we saw in chapter 2, this was an objection fired at Paul especially by Jewish Christians who felt that he was standing morality on its head, by offering righteousness before God to Gentiles apart from the law. How can rejection of the law lead to righteousness? In their eyes, it could only lead to law-lessness (in both senses). And in particular, they felt that Paul was undermining God's relationship to Israel: how could it be just for him to 'bring his wrath' against Israel on the basis of the law, if he were going to ignore the law completely in his treatment of the Gentiles?

'Why does God still blame us?' expresses this very thought. And this gives it a more precise meaning than appears at first sight. The objection is not a general philosophical comment, but is related to the particular understanding of Israel and the law which Paul's Jewish-Christian opponents had. In essence, the 'objector' is saying that Paul wrecks God's covenant relationship with Israel, by teaching that he has mercy on, or hardens, whomever he pleases (9:18). It seems to mean that God exercises the freedom *not* to show the mercy which, according to the covenant, he has pledged himself to show. The 'covenants' and 'promises' (9:4) are worth nothing, after all. So if God does not stick to them, how can he justly pass judgment on the basis of covenant law?

This is a substantial objection. And we can really sympathize with it. For at the heart of 'Israel theology' today is this very thought, that God cannot take back what he has once given. By teaching that God makes distinctions between individuals within the chosen people, Paul seems to undermine this covenant commitment.

How will he respond? At first sight, he seems to concede his objector's whole case, by comparing God to a potter who can do whatever he likes with the clay under his hand (v. 21). Professor C. H. Dodd, whose commentary on Romans is famous for its often highly critical attitude to Paul, remarks that Paul does indeed turn God into a 'non-moral despot' here, and objects, 'The trouble is that man is not a pot; he *WILL* ask, 'Why did you make me like this?', and he will not be bludgeoned into silence. It is the weakest point in the whole epistle.'

But, as usual with Paul, it is wrong to jump to hasty conclusions. He does not, I believe, make God a 'non-moral despot'. In fact he drops a hint about his response in the very way in which he phrases the imagined objection in verse 19, because 'For who resists his will?' is actually a quotation from the book of Job[1] (taken from the mouth of Job himself), and then Paul goes on to echo the language of Job further in his own challenge, 'Who are you, O man, to talk back to God?' (v. 20a). This sudden reminiscence of the book of Job is not accidental. In fact, the message of Job is vital for Paul's argument here.

---

[1] The verse quoted is Job 9:19, but English readers will be puzzled to find that it bears little relation to Paul's version of it here. In fact Paul quotes the Septuagint version of the verse, which itself is not an accurate translation of the Hebrew, although it well represents the overall meaning of that whole passage in Job. (The Septuagint was the Greek translation of the Old Testament current at the time of the New Testament.) Paul has also introduced one or two small changes into the quotation, which make it even more difficult for English readers looking up the verse. It would probably be better to call it an allusion, rather than a quotation, but Paul means us to spot it. He always assumed detailed knowledge of the Old Testament in his readers. The sensitive Bible student would also be aware that the word translated 'talk back to' in Rom. 9:20, an unusual and rather rare Greek word, is used specially in the Septuagint version of Job, to describe the attitude that Job himself took up towards God. (Out of five appearances of the word in the Old Testament, four of them are in Job.)

This is typical of the way Paul writes. It would be very easy to pass over these gentle allusions to Job (all the commentators on my shelf except one apparently fail to see them), and yet they shape the whole argument. Paul returns to the book of Job in 11:35, in the doxology with which he concludes Rom. 9 – 11, and clearly feels that, in wrestling with the problem of Israel, he is facing an issue of theodicy akin to that which tormented Job.

Learning to live like Job

Paul feels that the objector is in the same position as Job. That poor man was tortured by the sense that God had treated him unjustly, and yet he could not get near enough to God to plead his own cause and to complain. In the chapter to which Paul alludes, he cries out,

> *His wisdom is profound, his power is vast. Who has resisted him and come out unscathed? . . . How then can I dispute with him? How can I find words to argue with him? . . . Even if I summoned him and he responded, I do not believe he would give me a hearing. He would crush me with a storm . . .* (Jb. 9:4, 14, 16–17)

The sheer greatness of God oppresses Job, for what can he, a mere mortal, do when God by definition has all the answers and controls everything? By reminding us of Job's predicament, however, Paul undoubtedly wants us also to think of the answer which Job ultimately received. For the amazing thing is that, in the end, it was precisely the greatness of God which became the resolution of the problem. The book reaches a marvellous climax with a stunning self-revelation by God (chs. 38 – 41), in which he simply parades before Job the power, wisdom and mystery with which he has made the world and now governs it.

That was what Job had wanted to question: God was not governing it wisely, as far as he was concerned. At the end of the book he is silenced, but not because God has crushed him into submission, as he feared in chapter 9. Rather, he realizes that, if we freely submit to this God, a God who manages his creation with a wisdom far surpassing anything that we can grasp, then our rights are absolutely safe with him. He will not violate them. 'My ears had heard of you but now my eyes have seen you. Therefore I despise myself and repent in dust and ashes,' he prays (42:5–6). He regrets his 'talking back' to God, because it arose from ignorance of the true dimensions of God's greatness.

So when Paul tells his objector not to 'talk back' to God

(v. 20a), he is not abruptly dismissing the objection as an impertinence before the Creator. God did not dismiss Job like that, but commended him for his honesty (Jb. 42:7). The commentators interpret these verses as though Paul were simply poking his objector in the eye, and are fond of quoting the remark of the German Reformer Philip Melanchthon, who said that Paul simply 'breaks off the conversation' here, because there is a point beyond which creaturely curiosity may not pry. We may agree that there comes a point at which the answers to our questions will exceed our capacity to understand, but is it wrong to ask them, for that reason?

In fact Paul is telling his Jewish-Christian objector that the honest expression of his concern for Israel is natural, and right, and that if he will be open to God as Job was, he will learn the same lesson, and be led, like Job, to 'see' the God about whom as yet he has only 'heard' (Jb. 42:5). He needs to realize that the very moral sense which sometimes leads us to question God's actions is something implanted in us by him. How could we possibly, therefore, be more just than he? By definition, whatever he does is just – and praiseworthy. Our objections are caused by our poor eyesight. We need to catch a glimpse of the justice that impels him, a justice of mercy to the undeserving. It's *great* being a pot in his hands!

Like clay in his hands

And so we come to the metaphor of the potter and the pots in verse 20b–24. It is important to notice the way Paul bases his response to the objection on four rhetorical questions.

1. Verse 20a, 'Who are you . . . to talk back to God?' We have already thought how this focuses on the idea of creaturely submission to the Creator's wisdom. Questions 2, 3 and 4 follow on:

2. Verse 20b, 'Shall what is formed say to him who formed it . . .' presents the impossibility of the creature directing the work of the Creator.

3. Verse 21, 'Does not the potter have the right . . .' adds the thought of the authority of the Creator to do whatever he wills with his creation.

4. Verses 22–24, 'What if God . . .' (these verses are really one question, divided into two by the NIV) apply these principles to the problem of Israel and suggest – apparently – that the division within Israel between faith and unbelief is God's creation, for the sake of the church.

We must let Paul be as bold and forthright as he wants: the conclusion towards which he is heading in the last question seems dramatic indeed. On his way there, it is important to underline what he is not saying by his use of this metaphor of the potter. He is not teaching that, as far as God is concerned, human beings are as disposable as insentient pots. The point of comparison (and this is where Professor Dodd goes wrong, in the comment quoted above) is not in the objects made, but in the act of creation. Just as a human potter has complete power over what he makes, and can determine not only the shape of each pot but also the use to which each will be put, so God has the absolute right to shape and manage each creature of his exactly as he wills. To want anything else is to want God not to be God; it is to be like those who 'go to great depths to hide their plans from the Lord, who do their work in darkness and think, "Who sees us? Who will know?" ' (Is. 29:15). Isaiah's message for those who want to assert their autonomy from God in this way is crystal clear:

> *You turn things upside down, as if the potter were thought to be like the clay! Shall what is formed say to him who formed it, 'He did not make me'? Can the pot say of the potter, 'He knows nothing'?* (Is. 29:16)

This is the verse which Paul quotes here in Romans 9:20b. (See also Is. 45:9.) Of course, Dodd is right to sense that this potter-pot metaphor could easily be taken to down-grade human dignity and responsibility, and the problem of reconciling this sort of divine sovereignty with real human responsibility is indeed great. Fortunately, we do not have to solve that problem here, because it is not part of Paul's discussion but arises out of philosophical reflection on what he writes. (However, there is a brief discussion of the problem in a note at the end of this chapter.)

So verses 22–24 form the climax as Paul applies this understanding of God and the world to the problem of Israel and the church. We must seek to be as careful here as we can. It is misleading of the NIV to use the translation 'objects' in verse 22 for the same Greek word which it translates 'pottery' in verse 21. The thought of the potter runs right through the whole paragraph. (In fact the NIV should not have put in a paragraph division between verses 21 and 22 – Paul's thought runs right on.) So, although a little odd, the Revised Standard Version translation 'vessels of wrath' is probably better than 'the objects of his wrath'.

Questions beginning 'What if . . . ?' are usually followed by a statement starting with 'Then . . .'. ('What if it rains tomorrow? Then we'll have to hold the party indoors!') But here, Paul never gets around to the 'then' which his 'What if . . . ?' implies. So the first task is to decide what 'then'-clause is lurking at the back of his mind. Probably, it is '. . . then you have no reason to object like this!' Paul is still rebuffing the charge of injustice, in defence of his view that Israel's apostasy is within God's plan.

The second thing is to decide what 'choosing to show his wrath and make his power known' means (v. 22). Again, the NIV is misleading here. 'Choosing' implies to us that the thing chosen is put into effect. A trivial illustration makes this clear. 'Which will madam choose?', says the waiter with the sweet-trolley. Averting her eyes from the cream-smothered profiter-oles and cheesecake, madam reluctantly replies, 'I'll choose the fruit salad,' and does her waistline a lot of good. 'Choosing' means opting for one of two or more possibilities. And so, in verse 22, 'choosing' would suggest that, faced with the alternatives of showing his wrath or not showing it, God decided to show it.

But that is precisely what Paul says God did *not* do. He 'bore with great patience the "vessels of wrath" – prepared for destruction'. In other words, although they were 'fully fitted for destruction' (this would be a more literal translation), God decided *not* to execute his wrath on them, but 'bore' them instead.

This problem is entirely of the NIV's making. In fact Paul does not use the word 'choose' at all, but simply the word 'want' or 'will'. Tucking into her fruit salad, madam could not help her gaze straying over to the trolley in the corner, groaning under all that forbidden cream. She chose one, but she wanted the other. The illustration is trite, but the same principle applies here. In part at any rate, this verse presents us with something that God wanted to do but chose not to do.

This is very important. For in fact, 'showing his wrath' and 'making his power known' conflict with each other, as we have already seen in the case of Pharaoh in verse 17. God put off 'showing his wrath' against Pharaoh, because he intended to 'make his power known' by showing mercy to Israel – and thus to use Pharaoh as a means of writing a story which would be told world-wide, the story of his merciful election and deliverance of Israel. He could not both give Pharaoh what he deserved and express his mercy as he wanted to. Putting the same thing in terms of the potter, Pharaoh was a 'vessel of wrath' whom God 'bore with great patience' because he wanted 'to make the riches of his glory known to the "vessels of mercy" ' (v. 23).

Israel – a 'vessel of mercy'?

As a comment about the exodus, Paul's objector would have no difficulty at all with this. He too would be eager to teach that Pharaoh was a 'vessel of wrath' and Israel a 'vessel of mercy', and that God used Pharaoh as an object-lesson for the rest of the world. No-one, after the exodus, could doubt the Lord's determination to save and protect his people. The objector would also be more than keen to say that Israel had been 'prepared in advance for glory': the Lord had chosen her out of all the nations on earth, and brought her to himself, to reveal his glory to her and to dwell in her midst. This is what Paul himself says about Israel in 9:4. The trouble is, in these verses Paul is picturing Israel not as the 'vessel of mercy', but as the 'vessel of wrath'. He thinks of the 'vessels of mercy' as another group altogether – 'even us, whom he also called, not only from the Jews but also from the Gentiles' (v. 24). This is absolutely staggering.

It is not difficult, when this becomes clear, to imagine the raw hatred which Paul inspired against himself in some circles. To some Jewish Christians, he seemed to be trampling on the most holy things, rejecting the covenant itself. But there can be no doubt about what he teaches here, however reluctant they, or we, may be to accept it. Israel stands in the same position as Pharaoh, under a suspended or postponed judgment, while God extends mercy to the church of Christ, 'even us'.

The phrase 'whom he also called' in verse 24 points us to the basis of Paul's argument. He is in fact simply arguing from experience. Whatever understanding one may have of the covenant with Israel, he is saying, the fact simply has to be accepted that God has 'called' a people into being which consists of Jews and Gentiles together, with no distinction. This fact alone shows that God himself does not operate with an understanding of the old covenant which preserves that distinction between Jews and Gentiles. Paul then applies the same principle – the argument from experience – to Israel's unbelief. If it has happened, then it must be part of God's plan, and we have to accept it and shape our understanding of the covenant to match the facts, however difficult this may be.

But this reshaping cannot involve an overthrow of the Old Testament, for it is God's Word. Can Paul reconcile his viewpoint with the teaching of the Old Testament? His 'objectors' answered with an emphatic 'No!' But he was no mean Bible student; and in the next section he introduces a string of quotations by which he seeks to show that the present situation accords with the way God has always dealt with his people. He rejects his opponents' essentially sentimental interpretation of the Old Testament and the covenant with Israel, which regarded God as a constitutional monarch, simply signing all the bills sent to him and unquestioningly underwriting Israel's existence. No, insists Paul, he is an executive monarch, managing his people as he wills within the framework of his promises, even if this means making decisions hard for his subjects to understand.

No-one can doubt his courage, to maintain such teaching in the teeth of the opposition it provoked. But in the long run, as he wrestles with the Scriptures through these three intense chapters, we learn to admire not just his boldness but also the amazing deftness of his touch as a theologian and thinker. It is as easy today as it was then to misunderstand him or to jump to hasty conclusions about his teaching – and there are plenty of scholars today who feel that Paul's mind was a tissue of contradictory impulses. But once let him speak for himself, and a profound consistency emerges.

Additional note

Sovereignty and responsibility – thorns galore

Romans 9, along with Romans 8:31–39, is the passage above all to which Christians turn when the vexed question of predestination comes up. We have all had arguments about it. It usually starts when some bright spark remarks, 'If God's got everything decided in advance, what's the use of doing anything at all? For instance, if he's decided who are going to become Christians, what's the use of preaching the gospel?' And then the argument develops, usually involving at some point poor Judas Iscariot – 'Surely Judas didn't have any choice about betraying Jesus, because it's prophesied in the Old Testament that he will do it! That's unfair!'

The basic problem that always lies at the heart of discussions like this is the following. The Bible pictures God as absolutely in charge of his world, as its Creator and Governor. But the Bible also makes man thoroughly responsible for his own actions, so that he can justly be rewarded or blamed as appropriate. How can both be true? It is very hard to see how, if God is as completely in control of the world as the Bible teaches, any real responsibility for action can be allowed to man. Yet the Bible holds the two ideas alongside each other, and Judas Iscariot is a clear example of this. He bore the consequences of his decision to betray Jesus, and yet that betrayal had been determined long beforehand. Philosophically speaking, is this possible? Do we not ultimately have to choose between a sovereign God and a responsible man? Can we have both in one universe?

Some scholars feel that this is the problem which Paul tackles in Romans 9. They suggest that this is one of the few passages in the Bible where this difficulty is recognized and an answer given. Sadly, however, this is not the case. I do not think the Bible ever tackles this philosophical question, as such. Certainly it is not the problem which is occupying Paul in Romans 9. We know only too well what that is – the agonizing problem of squaring up Israel's collapse with God's promise that she would be his for ever. But it is easy to see how some have felt that Paul does indeed have the broader, more philosophical problem in mind here. For these are the underlying issues: the sovereignty of God (over the destiny of Israel) on the one hand, and the responsibility of man (for his self-exclusion from God's blessings) on the other.

You can't have it both ways!

If Paul comes so close to it, why does he not bring these underlying issues to the surface, since they are of such importance? Applying the Judas Iscariot problem to the whole of Israel, we could say to him, 'Paul, you must say either that Israel excludes herself from grace and is justly punished for her wilful rebellion, or that God will override her rebellion and save her regardless, but you can't have it both ways. If Judas were justly punished for betraying Jesus, then God can't have foreordained that Jesus would be betrayed.' But Paul clearly does not feel the problem like this. The nearest he comes to posing this question is in 9:19, when his imaginary objector jumps in with Job's charge of injustice and 'answers back' to God. For Job was in effect charging God with exercising his sovereignty in a way which denied his own humanity and responsibility. He felt that he had fully followed the Lord, and did not deserve such treatment.

So Paul's response to the objector is significant, because he would probably respond very similarly if we were able to put the Judas Iscariot problem to him direct. In all likelihood he would reply, 'Who do you think you are, to answer back to

God?' (9:20). As we saw above, this reference to Job does not mean that Paul is simply telling his objector to stop objecting because his question is improper. It is a proper question, but it must be answered as Job's question was. What Job needed was a new trust – trust that, whatever the appearance, his rights were perfectly safe in God's hands, for he would act with perfect wisdom and justice. What Job 'sees' at the end of the book is not a theoretical answer to his problem which justifies his responsibility as he wanted. Rather, he simply sees that, God being God, there is no need any longer to 'answer back'. He learns to trust the God whom he had previously charged with injustice.

We can be fairly sure that Paul would say the same about the 'Judas Iscariot' problem. He would not forbid us to seek a philosophical resolution of it, but he would tell us that in the long run the best answer is trust – in this case, a trust that God is quite capable of preserving man's integrity as a responsible being, even in a world which is fully determined by his providence. To suggest that we must choose between his sovereignty and our responsibility is to limit his power as Creator.

The glories and mysteries of creation, displayed so movingly before Job's astonished eyes as God's response to his 'answering back' (Jb. 38 – 41), speak to us in the same way. We too must reply, 'Not we!' to the grand succession of questions which God throws at Job, in spite of our much-vaunted twentieth-century science:

> *Have you ever given orders to the morning? . . . Can you take them [light and darkness] to their places? . . . Can you bind the beautiful Pleiades? . . . Do you know the laws of the heavens?* (Jb. 38:12, 20, 31, 33 – just a random selection)

Our own ignorance and child-likeness in the face of the world about us compel us to accept the fact that God really has made human beings responsible and free, without for one moment abdicating the throne of the universe. And accepting this will mean rejoicing in it as well.

A sovereignty that swamps responsibility?

Chapter five began with a phrase quoted from the Penguin Commentary on Romans by Professor J. C. O'Neill, in which he criticizes Paul for proposing 'a thoroughly immoral doctrine' in this part of Romans. Professor O'Neill is by no means the only one who objects like this. The objection is, of course, lodged on behalf of man: Paul is robbing man of his proper dignity and responsibility by teaching that God determines his eternal destiny without regard for human deserving – turning man into an insentient pot, as C. H. Dodd comments (see above, page 59). And it must be admitted that Romans 9 has sometimes been used to support a view of God which is more Moslem than Christian, teaching that he determines his world so absolutely that man really is not much different from a pot.

But O'Neill's charge is completely misplaced. If Paul really did believe that God's sovereignty wipes out all human responsibility, leaving man no capacity to determine his own life, then the apostasy of Israel would never have troubled him. His attitude would have been (putting it vividly), 'Never mind if Israel is not responding to the gospel at the moment! God has other ideas, and his will is bound to prevail. His time hasn't come yet!' In fact he is torn with agony over Israel's rejection of Christ, because he knows that her eternal destiny really is at stake. The depth of this agony is the measure of the significance he attaches to human will and responsibility. Israel has the power to deprive herself of the enjoyment of God's covenant. To accuse this Paul of an absolute determinism is completely misjudged.

A responsibility that swamps sovereignty?

But at the same time, we must also beware of going to the other extreme. A branch of modern theology, known as 'process theology', teaches that God is in a way part of his creation, growing with it, dependent on it, and as much determined by it as ruling it. God waits to see how it will all turn out, because built into the structure of the world is an enormous variable – the free will of man. How will he develop? Will he evolve more acceptable and God-like characteristics?

Or will he degenerate, prostitute his dignity with false gods? These theologians teach that the arrival of the kingdom of God has not been determined beforehand. We will get there eventually, because God is a great persuader, and he will ultimately manage to cajole us into true faith. But in the meantime God himself is as much a participant in the 'process' as man, seeking by his incarnation to involve himself wholly in the fickle and vacillating affairs of mankind.

This is a modern theological movement. But there have always been Christians who felt or taught that God waits in the wings for man to make the vital decisions, so that he can act accordingly. Having done all he can to provide a way of salvation, they say, God leaves it to us to decide whether or not to opt in – just as he allows the innocent to be the prey of the wicked in this world. Man's will is free – and so it must be undetermined.

Paul will not allow this either. You cannot read Romans 9 attentively, I believe, without feeling deeply the real responsibility which Paul allows to mankind: we have only ourselves to blame if we cut ourselves off from God's grace. But at the same time our responses are made in a world wholly determined by God, and the response of faith is born in us as a result of his decision to show mercy. He made such a decision when he extended mercy to Jacob and not to Esau, to Israel and not to Pharaoh, and he takes decisions like that on the same plane as all other decisions about his creation. He wills to act in this, and not in that, way, and we his creatures cannot gainsay him or deny him the right to do so. If, like Job, we feel we want to challenge the justice of this, then Paul will tell us that our trust in his power and wisdom is not sufficient. He can take decisions like that without violating our integrity as creatures made in his image, with wholly responsible wills of our own.

Glory be to . . . me?
This is the point at which the philosophers should take over. They will tell us either that Paul is living in Cloud-Cuckoo-Land, or that it is indeed possible to hold these two truths together as complementary and not contradictory. I am not

a philosopher and so I cannot attempt to judge what they might say. Our task is just to look at Paul, and about him we can say that he clearly feels no tension in holding both truths together.

In doing so, Paul is in harmony with the whole Bible. Examples could be multiplied of biblical passages in which this balance appears without any sense of contradiction. Let one suffice: Isaiah 10, a passage from which Paul quotes in Romans 9. In prophesying the assault of the Assyrians upon Israel, Isaiah emphasizes that they are the instruments of God's judgment: 'the rod of my anger, in whose hand is the club of my wrath! I send him against a godless nation . . .' (Is. 10:5f.). But Isaiah also prophesies God's judgment upon the Assyrians, precisely for carrying out the murderous series of invasions which brought them to the gates of Jerusalem. They did it in pride, in a spirit of violent imperialism – so God will cut Assyria down. In fact, this is the main burden of the prophecy (Is. 10:5–19). Unjust?

We can also say that this balance between the two accords with universal Christian experience. For no believer, looking back on the process by which he or she came to true Christian commitment, finds it natural to say, 'How marvellous that I had the strength to make the right decision and turn to Christ.' The prayer that springs naturally to our lips is, 'Praise be to the God and Father of our Lord Jesus Christ, who has blessed us in the heavenly realms with every spiritual blessing in Christ' (Eph. 1:3). As we look back, all the credit goes to God for reaching out to us in mercy and love. But at the time, we could well have been unaware of his hand upon us, and certainly we were taking steps by our own conscious volition. We were not acting against our will, of course – far from it. To be forced to believe would indeed violate our integrity. Rather, we were gladly and freely embracing the grace of God in Christ. The philosophical problem is posed by our own experience, not just by Romans 9.

Personally, I find this tension very easy to live with. I do not lie awake at night wondering how on earth I can reconcile divine sovereignty with human responsibility, because somehow, in God's world, it is simply natural both to trust him to lead us along the path which he has planned for us, and to be joyfully determined to stick to that path come what may. Paul knew that only God, by his Holy Spirit, could fit us for his presence (1 Thes. 5:23). But at the same time he could labour as if the whole work of sanctification depended on him: 'We proclaim him, admonishing and teaching everyone with all wisdom, so that we may present everyone perfect in Christ' (Col. 1:28). We are not surprised to find in the very next verse another extraordinary paradox: 'To this end I labour, struggling with all *his* energy, which so powerfully works in me' (Col. 1:29). Sometimes it is hard to give a complete intellectual description of something which we intuitively sense as Christians – because we worship 'in spirit and in truth' (Jn. 4:23), encountering God as whole people, and not just as enquiring minds. Once again, we realize how natural it is that Romans 9 – 11 closes with a doxology (11:33–36).

CHAPTER SEVEN

God's word for Israel

[25]*As he says in Hosea:*

'I will call them "my people" who are not my
people;
and I will call her "my loved one" who is not my loved one,'

[26]*and,*

'It will happen that in the very place where it was said to them,
"You are not my people,"
they will be called "sons of the living God".'

[27]*Isaiah cries out concerning Israel:*

'Though the number of the Israelites be like the sand by the
sea,
only the remnant will be saved.
[28]*For the Lord will carry out*
his sentence on earth with speed and finality.'

[29]*It is just as Isaiah said previously:*

'Unless the Lord Almighty
had left us descendants,
we would have become like Sodom,
we would have been like Gomorrah.'

(Romans 9:25–29)

This passage carries straight on from the last. It is in fact misleading to separate it off as we have done here. 'As he says in Hosea' introduces the much-needed scriptural proof of the amazing things that Paul has just said. He has actually taught that Israel – at any rate, in part – can now be called a 'vessel of wrath, prepared for destruction' as far as God is concerned. Shocking though it is, this is certainly how his opponents would have read verses 22–24, and this in itself is an argument for the rightness of this interpretation. It is therefore absolutely imperative that Paul should justify his argument from the Old Testament.

He has also, in typical fashion, just slipped in the thought of the inclusion of the Gentiles in God's people (in v. 24). This was another huge bone of contention between him and his opponents, as we saw in chapter two, and he will tackle this issue with gusto in Romans 10. He prepares the way for that discussion here, by introducing the thought in advance. And having introduced it, he needs to give it some Old Testament support as well, again in a preliminary way which looks forward to the next section.

These verses are just a string of Old Testament quotations. Verses 25–26 are from Hosea, a combination of Hosea 2:23 and 1:10 (in that order). Verses 27–28 come from Isaiah 10:22–23, perhaps suggested to Paul's mind because the first part of Hosea 1:10, which he does not quote, also compares the Israelites to the sand on the seashore, like Isaiah 10:22. And finally, verse 29 is a quotation of Isaiah 1:9. As we examine these quotations, we have two vital questions in mind. Firstly, How do these quotations from the prophets provide support for Paul's argument? And secondly, because they are especially important and bring this whole section of Romans to a climax, we must also ask, Is Paul being true to the Old Testament in the way he uses them? These questions set the agenda for our thoughts in this chapter.

Hosea – the prophet of restoration and love (verses 25–26)

In his experience with his unfaithful wife Gomer, Hosea mirrored the relationship between Israel and the Lord: like the Lord, he suffered all the pain of rejection and the hurt of a love which goes on burning, however much wounded. He went and rescued his wife and took her back, to picture how the Lord was determined to draw Israel back to himself, in spite of her sin and rebellion.

Hosea was also commanded by God to give his children symbolic names, to act as signs to Israel. And so two of them had to bear the dreadful names 'Lo-Ruhamah' and 'Lo-Ammi', which meant 'Not-loved' and 'Not-mine' (literally, 'Not-my-people'. See Hos. 1:6–9). It is not hard to imagine the stigma borne constantly by a girl with the name 'Not-loved'. People knew her father was a prophet, and the message went home: Israel is a child rejected by God.

But after a while a symbolic name-changing ceremony took place: 'Say of your brothers, "My people", and of your sisters, "My loved one" ' (Hos. 2:1). The message of the change was just as clear, a message summarized in the verses which Paul quotes: the Lord will recreate the broken relationship, even though all the unfaithfulness was on Israel's side and the inevitable consequences must be suffered.

Paul felt that this prophecy was being fulfilled in his own day, through the creation of the church. And undoubtedly he felt that an even greater fulfilment was taking place than that envisaged by Hosea, for among the 'not-my-people' who are being 'called my people' were many Gentiles, brought into the sphere of God's people for the first time.

In fact, most of the commentators think that this re-naming of the Gentiles is the whole point of the quotation of Hosea here. They suggest that it relates only to the last phrase in verse 24, '. . . but also from the Gentiles'. This would not be the first time that Paul found hints of a thoroughly respectable Old Testament idea in a place where it was not originally intended. Many passages in the Old Testament do indeed promise the bringing-in of the Gentiles into God's people, and Paul quotes several of them elsewhere in Romans.

I do not find this a wholly satisfying interpretation, however, for the thought of the inclusion of the Gentiles is just a passing one in verse 24. Paul will turn to it properly in the next section. Since both he and Hosea had Israel primarily in mind, it is better to interpret his quotation in line with his main thrust. In any case, it is one thing to find unintended ideas hinted at in an Old Testament text, but quite another to interpret that text in a sense directly opposite to the original.

So it is probably truer to say that Paul has the whole of verse 24 in mind as he quotes Hosea: '. . . even us, whom he also called, not only from the Jews but also from the Gentiles'. He is saying that, in the 'calling' of Jews and Gentiles alike, by which the church of Jesus Christ has come into being, this prophecy of Hosea is being fulfilled.

We remember that 'calling' is something very special for Paul: it is the divine summons whereby we are drawn out of darkness into light, the touch of the Holy Spirit which brings us into fellowship with Christ: in addition to Romans 8:28, 30, see 1 Corinthians 1:9 and Galatians 1:6. Hosea did not, of course, have this sort of 'calling' in mind when he re-named his children. But Paul does not stretch the idea unduly, for Hosea too saw the re-'calling' of his own children as a picture of a restoration from hostility into harmony effective for God's whole people.

Paul used the idea of 'calling' at the beginning of his discussion, 9:7 (*cf.* 9:12); and by returning to it here he tells us that he is drawing the threads together and rounding off this first section of argument. In fact other terms used at the start also reappear in these verses, especially 'seed' (vv. 7–8, 29) and 'word' (vv. 6, 28 – translated 'sentence' by NIV). The fact that they bracket the section between them tells us that these are the leading themes in Paul's mind throughout, and so we pay special attention to what he says about them here.

This fulfilling of Hosea is very remarkable. Just when we expect Paul to produce a verse to support his sombre picture of Israel as a 'vessel of wrath', he turns to one full of hope and promise. Of course, it has a sombre background. Hosea and Paul have both delivered the awful message 'You are not my people' to the very people who fancied they were secure in God's favour. (We remember the start of Paul's argument in 9:6–7.) But now, also like Hosea, Paul seems to do an about-turn, has a name-changing ceremony, and tells Israel that God will restore her to her position once again, in association with the Gentiles.

The question that immediately occurs to us is, To what extent does this quotation actually limit or alter the meaning of verses 23–24? Paul introduces the quotation as though it will provide support for what he has just written, but it actually seems almost to contradict it. We could put the question in the way favoured by some scholars, and ask, Is Paul so emotionally attached as a Jew to his own nation, that he cannot resist acknowledging her special position in God's purposes, in spite of his own real denial of it? These scholars insist that the logic of Paul's argument is indeed to do what his opponents accused him of doing – to remove Israel from her privileged position as God's chosen race, and to substitute the church (composed of Jews and Gentiles together) as the heir of the promises. This, they say, is what Paul teaches in Romans 4:11f., 16, where he says that Abraham is the father of all who believe, whether Jews or Gentiles. This emphasis on faith, they suggest, and Paul's corresponding rejection of 'the works of the law', logically mean the termination of the covenant.

But, they go on, his own instincts as a Jew will not let him follow his logic rigorously to its conclusion, and so he draws back from the brink, and illogically continues to teach that Israel is God's elect people. Hence, they say, Paul prophesies the future salvation of Israel on the basis of the covenant with the patriarchs (11:26–28), although his gospel implicitly denies this possibility. And here in 9:25–26 the same process can be seen.

Could this be true? Of course we are all prey to our instincts, and it was precisely Paul's love of his fellow-Jews which made him feel their plight so deeply. But could his love for them have led him into such gross inconsistency? Actually, it is this Hosea quotation which gives the lie to this view. For if Paul is inconsistent in this respect, then so also was Hosea. But, so far as I know, no one has yet accused Hosea of illogicality in prophesying the restoration of Israel by God. In fact, the whole point of verses 22–24 is to tell us that there are indeed 'vessels of mercy' in Israel, and God has held back his judgment upon the nation in order that these 'vessels' may get to know 'the riches of his glory'. While wrath is delayed, mercy is extended, and Paul sums this whole process up in Hosea's terms as a re-'calling', a summoning of the nation back to what she should be, in Christ: 'sons of the living God'.

But Israel is to share this blessing with the Gentiles. They too are to hear this re-'calling' from God. In the Gentiles' case, the word 'You are not my people' has been directed at them ever since the Lord called Abraham to leave Ur and thus chose Israel for himself (Gn. 12:1–3). In the case of the Jews, 'You are not my people' is a horrifying word of judgment borne out of awful disobedience and rebellion. But in both cases there is to be restoration.

Paul leaves it at that for the moment. He has opened the window on to countryside which he will lead us to explore in chapter eleven. We need further preparation yet, if we are to be able rightly to interpret his ringing statement 'All Israel will be saved!', when eventually we come to it (11:26).

Isaiah – the prophet of judgment and hope (verses 27–29)

Isaiah was Paul's favourite prophet. He quotes from him on no fewer than nineteen occasions in Romans, twelve of them in chapters 9 – 11, equalling the number of quotations from the whole of the Pentateuch (the first five books of the Bible). And on five of these occasions, as here, Paul underlines the special significance of the quotation by introducing it by name. A double quotation from Isaiah, introduced twice by name, bringing this whole section of argument to a conclusion: Romans 9:27–29 is important indeed.

Verse 27 begins with a 'but' which the NIV has unfortunately omitted. Including it helps to clarify the flow of the argument.

For Isaiah is introduced to guard against the kind of mis-understanding we have just been considering. For we could conclude from Hosea that all was once again sweetness and light, that God had forgotten his wrath, and that the identi-fication with Pharaoh and the 'vessels of wrath' had all been a bad dream. Isaiah warns us not to be so hasty. To put the message of these quotations into a nutshell: God will keep all his words to Israel – his words of judgment on sin as well as those promising salvation and life. Israel is to be delivered, not from judgment, but through it: the very process of judg-ment on sin will be part of the means whereby he keeps his word to' Israel and brings her to salvation. This is a sad as well as a glorious message, as hard to hear today as it was then, but absolutely vital if we are really seeking Paul's guid-ance about the problem of Israel.

The first quotation takes us to another of the crises which Israel faced during her long history. The date is (almost certainly) 701 BC, the situation is the story told in 2 Kings 18:13 – 19:37 and Isaiah 37 – 38. Sennacherib, the king of Assyria, has invaded Judah and is threatening the very gates of Jerusalem. Isaiah is commissioned to speak a message of judgment: because the people have rebelled against the Lord, and placed their trust in worldly resources rather than in his strength, the Lord has raised up the Assyrians against them (Is. 37:22–29). But in this crisis Hezekiah, the king of Judah, turns to the Lord with heartfelt prayer (Is. 37:14–20), and the Lord hears his cry. So the message of judgment is balanced by one of hope. In Isaiah 10:20, immediately preceding the verses Paul quotes, we hear the promise,

> *In that day the remnant of Israel, the survivors of the house*
> *of Jacob, will no longer rely on him who struck them down*
> *but will truly rely on the Lord, the Holy One of Israel.*

(See also Isaiah 37:30–35.) This promise was followed by the deliverance described in 2 Kings 19:35–37 (also Isaiah 37:36–38), in which Sennacherib's army was struck by a decimating illness which wiped out his strength and compelled him to withdraw.

So Isaiah 10:22–23 (the verses which Paul actually quotes, rather freely) contains a message both of judgment and of hope. One word brings both halves of the message into focus together, the word 'remnant'. The NIV has misleadingly inserted the word 'only' before 'the remnant' in verse 27, which makes the emphasis fall on the tiny salvation contrasted to the great judgment which preceded it – 'only the remnant'! This thought may be at the back of Paul's mind, but his emphasis really falls on the certainty with which we may expect the salvation of the remnant. Because of God's just judgment on sin, Israel is reduced to a 'remnant' of her former size and glory, but the salvation of that remnant is just as sure as the judgment which sin inevitably provokes.

Verse 28 drives the point home. The word translated 'sentence' is actually 'word', the same as that which started off the whole section in verse 6: 'It is not as though God's word had failed'. Verse 28 is a statement of the certainty of the fulfilment of God's 'word' – he will 'carry it out with speed and finality'. But it is not the 'word' which Paul's objectors had in mind, when they accused him of overthrowing God's promises to Israel and making the Old Testament null and void. They were thinking simply of the promises of grace and blessing, the things which Paul himself lists in 9:4–5. He wants to remind them, very forcibly, that God's word to Israel was altogether more serious than simply a promise to bless her, come what may. The covenant laid great emphasis on Israel's responsibility to obey, and warned of awful judgment, if obedience were not forthcoming. This side of God's 'word' must be taken seriously, too.

Sodom and Gomorrah

This brings us to verse 29, with its quotation of Isaiah 1:9, which brings Romans 9 to a heart-rending conclusion. By its use of the word 'seed' (translated 'descendants' by NIV), this quotation also looks back to 9:7–8, and thus links in the idea of the 'remnant' with the argument of the whole chapter. Also, Isaiah 1:9 is a statement of principle, not related to a specific situation, like his own statement in 9:8 that 'it is not the natural children who are God's children, but it is the children of the promise who are regarded as Abraham's "seed" '. This is the significance of Paul's introduction, 'As Isaiah said previously': it points to the fact that, before ever the Assyrian crisis had loomed, God had stated it as a matter of principle that, in his dealings with Israel, there would inevitably be judgment, and that salvation would always be a privilege bestowed upon a 'seed', a remnant.

Sodom and Gomorrah represented paganism at its absolute worst: in the heinous lifestyle which separation from God produced, and then in the awful judgment which such a lifestyle provokes. Isaiah actually compares Israel to Sodom and Gomorrah – except for the difference that, when judgment falls on Israel, God leaves a 'seed' to be the focus of restoration and new life, just as, right from the very start of her existence, he has distinguished within her between those whom he regards as the 'children of promise', and those whose relationship to Abraham is purely physical and not spiritual as well. But here, unlike verse 27, the emphasis certainly falls on the contrast between what Israel should have been and what she has become. The verse before the one which Paul quotes contains a vivid picture: 'The Daughter of Zion is left like a shelter in a vineyard, like a hut in a field of melons, like a city under siege' (Is. 1:8).

Instead of being the glorious 'city set on a hill', shining like a beacon for all the nations, Jerusalem has become like a ramshackle shed in the middle of a field, tumbledown and insignificant.

Paul began with tears, and we can well imagine a few more spilling on to the page as he writes these lines. Sodom and Gomorrah! To compare Israel with these must have torn at his heart-strings. And yet the comparison is not his, but Isaiah's. And this is precisely the point he wants to make: his interpretation of Israel's failure as intended by God, in fulfilment of his just covenant dealings with her, must receive scriptural support if his opponents are to be diverted from dismissing Paul as a raving lunatic. So he shows how Isaiah says the same thing. Israel's glorious status as the people of God can be horribly changed, so that she can 'become' like

Sodom in God's eyes; and indeed this is the expected course of her history, announced 'previously', before any crisis of rebellion and judgment arose.

The issue at stake between Paul and his opponents boils down to the question, What is the relationship between judgment and salvation in God's dealings with Israel? They understood the covenant to mean that God had committed himself to Israel's salvation, so that his judgment was not a thing to fear. Conversely, when they heard Paul making statements of judgment like these in Romans 9 or elsewhere (for instance, 1 Thes. 2:16), they naturally accused him of preaching the termination of the covenant.

Paul did not regard things so simply. For him, the point was that the awful 'word' of judgment comes to Israel within the covenant. God would not be acting in judgment upon her, were it not that he had chosen Abraham and his seed for ever. Both 'words' must be fulfilled, if the covenant is to stand. The relevance of this to the debate about Israel today is clear. Some versions of the 'Israel theology' fall into the mistake made by Paul's opponents, and simply underline God's blanket, universal commitment to Israel. But Paul opposed this view, and so should we. We need to imitate his careful, discriminating attitude to the covenant.

In this respect Paul was more biblical than his opponents. There is an interesting parallel with the study of the book of Amos at this point. One particular school of Old Testament scholarship teaches that Amos was the first prophet actually to threaten Israel with the termination of the covenant, because of her sin and rebellion. Amos, they say, went further than his predecessors when he wrote (for instance), 'Fallen is Virgin Israel, never to rise again . . . Will not the day of the Lord be darkness, not light – pitch-dark, without a ray of brightness?' (Am. 5:2, 20; see also 8:14). There was no hope for Israel left. But other commentators rightly resist this depressing interpretation. They take the book as a whole, and interpret these horrifying predictions of judgment alongside the expressions of hope which the book contains, especially at the end (9:11–15). The first group has to cut these passages out as later additions, inconsistent with the original message.

But those who wish to retain the expressions of hope in Amos say that what he is proclaiming, in effect, is the seriousness of the covenant. Israel cannot take it for granted. If the Lord is serious about the judgment he inflicts upon his chosen people, he will also be serious about the promises of salvation, and vice versa. It may be that Amos had to major on the former, because of the circumstances of his ministry, but the latter are there as well. I am sure that this is the right approach, and that Paul is treating the covenant in precisely the same way in Romans 9.

Does Paul use the Old Testament acceptably here? His opponents would be keen to spot any misuse. Personally, I have no objections to raise. He seems to me fully and fairly to justify from the Old Testament the argument which comes to a climax here – even in his use of Hosea, beside which a question-mark is set by some of the commentators. The Old Testament will continue to feature largely in his argument, perhaps even more crucially as he turns in the next section to the other half of the problem, the inclusion of the Gentiles in God's people.

It is true that the tears are never far from the surface, as he pursues his course through this most tender subject, and we will not be able to interpret these chapters correctly unless we weep with him. But his feelings never get the better of his judgment, I believe. His use of the Old Testament is rigorous and careful, even in the next section where he has been charged with grave misuse. His Old Testament quotations are vital within his argument, and as we move into Romans 10 we will proceed as we have thus far: looking carefully at the total context of the passages he uses, while keeping a tight grip on the development of his argument from step to step.

CHAPTER EIGHT

Believing Gentiles, unbelieving Jews, and God's law

Another main section of Romans 9 – 11 begins in 9:30. 'What then shall we say?' shows that Paul is standing back from what he has just written, and drawing conclusions from it. Because these conclusions are so mind-boggling, they naturally become the starting-point for further discussion in chapter 10.

Once again he marks the extent of a section of argument by beginning and ending it on the same note. Both 9:30–31 and 10:20–21 contrast the Gentiles' unexpected entry into salvation with Israel's failure and rebellion. In 10:20–21, once again, Paul does not use his own words but quotes from Isaiah – so that this section, like the last, ends with a double, ascribed quotation from Paul's favourite Old Testament book.

These structural signals are deliberate, I believe, and help us to understand Paul's meaning by enabling us to survey the countryside before we cross it. By beginning and ending with this contrast, Paul is quietly giving us his own chapter-heading for this section. And by using two verses from Isaiah to express the contrast at the end, he makes it clear that, once again, he is going to be concerned throughout to root his discussion in the Old Testament.

Three 'new' themes

The section 9:30 – 10:21 is marked by the appearance of three themes which have never been far from our minds, but which were not actually mentioned in the last section.

84

First, Jesus reappears. He was not mentioned at all in 9:6–29, although he was the unspoken presupposition of all that Paul wrote. But now, by the 'stone' quotation from Isaiah in 9:33, by the teasing statement in 10:4 ('Christ is the end of the law . . .'), and by the discussion of what it means to confess 'Jesus is Lord' (10:5–13), Paul once again focuses his whole discussion around him.

Secondly, 'the law' is brought specifically into the discussion. Paul has written about this at length earlier in Romans; and although he has already (in 8:1–4) taken a step towards justifying his claim that he does not 'overthrow the law' by his doctrine of faith, but rather 'establishes' it (3:31, AV), it is really in this section that he brings the law and Christ into relationship with each other. What he says here about the law is of crucial importance for us as we try to weigh up the claims of 'Israel theology'. (The NIV is misleading in 9:31 when it uses the expression 'a law': Paul is referring to *the* law, the law of Moses in which Israel trusted.)

The third new factor is the theme of 'righteousness'. The Greek word appears no fewer than eleven times in this section, eight of them in 9:30 – 10:4. It too has been a major subject earlier in the letter. In fact many regard it as the central theme of Romans. English readers need to be aware of the fact that we have to use two English words ('righteousness' and 'justification') to cover Paul's use of just one Greek word. His doctrine of 'justification', therefore, is in fact a doctrine of 'righteousness', and so what he writes here in 9:30ff. builds upon his teaching on that theme in chapters 2 – 6.

These three themes are closely connected to each other. 'Righteousness' and 'the law' were the issues central to the disagreement between Paul and his opponents. He and they were simply giving different answers to the question, 'How does man find righteousness in the sight of God?' For his opponents, the answer was clear from the Old Testament: man must tread God's prescribed way of righteousness, accepting the 'yoke of the law' signified by circumcision – and this applies to Gentiles as well as Jews, both before and after Christ. But Paul insisted,

We maintain that a man is justified by faith apart from observing the law. God . . . will justify the circumcised by faith and the uncircumcised through that same faith (Rom. 3:28, 30)

– and that faith is Christian faith. His opponents saw things in black and white terms: you could either have a real, biblical righteousness on God's terms, based on his law and crowned by his Messiah, or you could have the spurious righteousness offered by Paul – which was no righteousness, because it rejected the law.

But matters were more complicated than this. In one sense, of course, Paul did indeed reject the law. We saw in chapter two how, at his conversion, he turned from the law to Christ. Notice 'apart from observing the law' in the quotation above. But, on the other hand, Paul's whole discussion here starts from the claim that the word of God has not failed (9:6). He would not make this claim, were he not convinced that the law really was upheld and vindicated in Christ. In fact he attempts something very bold indeed in this section of Romans: he seeks to prove from the law itself that righteousness comes by faith in Christ alone, so that the law actually demotes itself to second place. As he puts it in Galatians 2:19, 'through the law I died to the law'. He attempts to show that the law itself requires faith in Christ for righteousness.

This means that Paul's use of the Old Testament is especially crucial in this section, and we shall have to concern ourselves again with the question, Does Paul use his quotations fairly? For quite a few modern scholars have sided with his ancient opponents, and have accused him of failing miserably to prove that his gospel does not mean the rejection of the law. To support their accusation, they point to what they think is the very shady way in which Paul treats the Old Testament in this section, particularly in 10:5–8. The only way he can get the Old Testament on his side, they argue, is to make it say the opposite of what it really means. We shall face their accusations when we get to 10:5–8.

And so we turn to the first paragraph of this section.

The law — lost and found

> [30]*What then shall we say? That the Gentiles, who did not pursue righteousness, have obtained it, a righteousness that is by faith;* [31]*but Israel, who pursued a law of righteousness, has not attained it.* [32]*Why not? Because they pursued it not by faith but as if it were by works. They stumbled over the 'stumbling-stone.'* [33]*As it is written:*
>
> *'See, I lay in Zion a stone that causes men to stumble*
> *and a rock that makes them fall,*
> *and the one who trusts in him will never be put to shame.'*
>
> (Romans 9:30–33)

The submarine's superstructure and deck emerges. Previously only the periscope was seen, at 9:24 when Paul suddenly mentioned the Gentiles. But now it becomes clear that a large body was lurking under the surface at that point, ready to appear. Drawing the conclusion from what he has just written, Paul immediately mentions the Gentiles again, and contrasts them with the Jews.

In verse 30 he is simply stating a fact, which he hopes no-one will dispute, friend or foe: there has been a great influx of Gentiles into the fellowship of God's people. The gift of the Holy Spirit to Gentile believers was an undeniable fact, which simply had to be accepted even by those who felt that the Holy Spirit had acted most rashly and untheologically. We saw in chapter two how Romans can be thought of as Paul's attempt to explain and vindicate this action of the Holy Spirit in conformity with the Old Testament, so as to make it easier for Jewish Christians to accept (see above, p. 24). He underlines the facts: 'the Gentiles, who did not pursue righteousness, have obtained it'! And they obtained it 'by faith', that is, simply by believing the message about Jesus, and not by submitting to any ritual or religious system.

Israel, on the other hand, has moved in the opposite direction. The most important feature of verse 31 has been obscured by the NIV, in common with most other translations:

the 'it' at the end of the verse (in the phrase 'has not attained it') refers not to 'righteousness' but to 'the law'. This makes Paul's statement very radical indeed. He is not just claiming that Israel has failed to attain righteousness (in contrast to the Gentiles). He is saying more than that: like a huntsman after his prey, Israel set out to catch the law, but it eluded her grasp. For all her devotion to the law, she has failed to tame it, failed to persuade it to yield up the prize it guards (righteousness), missed its inner purpose and meaning. So her failure to enjoy the righteousness which has been poured out on the Gentiles is not the essence of the problem, but merely a symptom of a deeper ill – her failure to understand what the law is and to discover the key that unlocks it.

Verse 32 gives the reason for this failure, and how amazing it is! The net with which Israel was trying to trap her prey (a 'hunting' metaphor runs right through these verses) was faulty. If she had tried to catch the law *by faith*, all would have been well. But instead she tried to catch it *by works*, and all that happened was that she fell over an unobserved rock lying on the path and came to grief. Her quarry got away. She should have heeded the prophet (Isaiah, of course) who said that it is the one who has faith who will not be shamed in the judgment day (v. 33). This quotation, a combination of Isaiah 8:14 and 28:16, is used elsewhere in the New Testament with specific reference to Jesus (see 1 Pet. 2:4–8 and compare Mt. 21:42 and Acts 4:11), and undoubtedly Paul is applying it to Jesus here. He is a stone which can either cause the downfall of one who stumbles against it, or become the rock of refuge for the one who rests his faith upon it.

Fulfilling the law – by faith

It is important to realize exactly what Paul is saying. Israel's failure to believe in Jesus (she has crashed into the rock, instead of building upon him) is equivalent to her failure to catch the law. In both cases she should have exercised faith, but did not. On the other hand, the Gentiles have had the required faith (in the rock), have therefore obtained righteousness and, we infer, have thus 'attained the law'. In each case, 'righteousness' and 'the law' go together. Those who have the one have the other also, whether they are Gentiles or Jews. Gentiles, who believe in Jesus, fulfil the law. It is a great pity that the translations obscure this vital aspect of Paul's argument here.

We immediately ask (with Paul's opponents), How could the Gentiles fulfil the law in ignorance of it? Is not this argument rather underhand? We can easily sympathize with Jewish Christians who felt that, if Jesus were the Messiah of Israel, then logically Gentiles should join Israel if they wanted him. But Paul rejects this, and goes on the offensive, boldly asserting that the only way to fulfil the law is to believe in Jesus, both for Jews and for Gentiles. (Of course he insisted that the Gentiles must get to know the Old Testament Scriptures, but not as a condition of salvation.) To find 'righteousness', they simply need to rest on the rock. Paul devotes 10:1–13 to justifying this outrageous assertion.

There is an important passage earlier in Romans which sheds light on Paul's meaning:

> *Circumcision has value if you observe the law, but if you break the law, you have become as though you had not been circumcised. If those who are not circumcised keep the law's requirements, will they not be regarded as though they were circumcised? The one who is not circumcised physically and yet obeys* [Greek 'fulfils'] *the law will condemn you who, even though you have the written code and circumcision, are a law-breaker.* (Rom. 2:25–27)

It is vital to realize that Paul is not saying here, 'If there ever should be a Gentile who keeps the law, then that person would be regarded as circumcised in God's sight.' Rather, he is thinking of an actual fulfilment of the law by Gentiles, who thus put Jews to shame. A few verses earlier, he wrote, 'When Gentiles, who do not have the law, do by nature things required by the law . . .' (2:14): 'when', not 'if'.

I believe that Paul is thinking of Gentile Christians in both places, although many commentators take a different view. Having condemned the whole Gentile world so unreservedly in Romans 1:18–32 for refusing to acknowledge and thank the God revealed in creation, it would surely be impossible for Paul to go on in chapter 2 to teach that pagan Gentiles, by their obedience to the light of their own consciences, are able to earn 'glory, honour and peace' at the final judgment day (2:10). A radical transformation has brought about a whole new obedience: 'the requirements of the law are written on their hearts' (2:15). This can only be transformation by the regenerating work of the Holy Spirit. Paul drops a hint to this effect in 2:29 when he refers to 'circumcision of the heart, by the Spirit'.

So just as the loss of circumcision is an awful reality for those who possess the physical mark but not its spiritual and moral outworking (2:25), so circumcision is gained by those who do not possess the physical mark, but who yet display – through Christ – the spiritual vigour which circumcision was meant to signal (2:26). They 'fulfil the law' (2:27). We are reminded of Philippians 3:3, where Paul, warning the Philippians against the Jews who persecuted him, exclaims, 'It is we who are the circumcision, we who worship by the Spirit of God, who glory in Christ Jesus.' Whether they were Jews or Gentiles by race (and the Philippians were undoubtedly a mixture), they had the right to regard themselves as the true bearers of the mark of God's people, because of their possession of the Holy Spirit. Paul's persecutors were merely 'mutilators of the flesh' (Phil. 3:2).

Two outrageous assertions

Paul's accusation (that Israel has not understood the law) is all of a piece with his constant use of the Old Testament throughout Romans 9 – 11. He wants to establish the correct way of understanding and interpreting the Old Testament over against those who interpret the covenant differently.

But in 9:30–33 he has given this thought a particular twist: for, secondly, he has actually taught that simply believing in Jesus is all that the law requires. In Paul's day there were many Gentiles who were attracted to the Jewish way of life and adopted some or all of its features. Many of the earliest Gentile converts came from the ranks of these 'God-fearers', as they were called. In their case it was not difficult for them to believe that their new faith in Israel's Messiah should lead them deeper into observance of Israel's law, and conversions of this sort were perfectly acceptable to Paul's opponents. But Paul specifically claims here that it was Gentiles 'who did not pursue righteousness' who have stumbled upon it. He is thinking here of the Gentiles to whom he had taken the gospel, those with an entirely pagan background, who had embraced Christ and found righteousness in him entirely without reference to the law (*cf.* 1 Thes. 1:9f.). In order to vindicate his ministry, Paul needs to prove this second point.

Paul tackles the first assertion (that Israel has not understood the law) in 10:1–4. The second (that the law tells us to believe in Christ) is the theme of 10:5–13.

Israel, the law and Christ

> *[1]Brothers, my heart's desire and prayer to God for the Israelites is that they may be saved. [2]For I can testify about them that they are zealous for God, but their zeal is not based on knowledge. [3]Since they did not know the righteousness that comes from God and sought to establish their own, they did not submit to God's righteousness. [4]Christ is the end of the law so that there may be righteousness for everyone who believes.* (Romans 10:1–4)

Unfortunately, NIV again lets us down. It has twice omitted the vital 'for', from the start of both verse 3 and verse 4. It is sadly prone to miss out these vital connecting words ('for', 'therefore', 'but', *etc.*), which are the oil which lubricates the flow of the meaning from verse to verse. Here, the omitted 'fors' tell us that verse 3 is intended to support and justify verse 2, and that verse 4 likewise explains verse 3. This is particularly important for the correct interpretation of the difficult but vital verse 4.

Paul reminds us of his heart-felt longing for Israel. His opponents must have easily assumed that his (to their mind) frightful attitude towards Israel arose from a basic heartlessness. So he takes every opportunity to bare his soul, and to show us the grief and the yearning he feels over her unbelief.

He longs and prays for her salvation, for he is as prepared as any to recognize and applaud her 'zeal' for God (v. 2). Anyone familiar with Jewish religious life, particularly amongst orthodox Jews, will know exactly what he means. But the grief arises because her zeal, although so intense, is 'not based on knowledge'. The particular Greek word Paul uses means 'knowledge with understanding' – perhaps 'insight' would be a better translation. For all her zealous attention to God's law, Israel has not attained real insight into it.

Christ, the end of the law

In verses 3 and 4 Paul seeks to justify this distressing accusation. It is important to remember that the opponents whom he is trying to convince are Jewish Christians, not just Jews. His argument is hardly one which would convince unbelievers. But it might well carry weight with someone already convinced that Jesus is the Messiah.

In essence, his argument is this: just as the law enshrines the righteousness of God for Israel, so Jesus is an expression of that same righteousness, in personal, living form. If the Jews had had true insight into God's righteousness in one form (the written), they would have recognized it in the other form as well (the personal). But they rejected Christ, and thus demonstrate that, for all their zeal for God, their knowledge of his righteousness is not real.

The 'for' at the start of verse 4 (in the Greek) shows how this is Paul's meaning: 'They did not submit to God's righteousness, for Christ is the end of the law. . . .' The word 'end' does not mean 'termination', as though Christ 'puts an end' to the law. Rather (I believe), it means 'terminus' in the sense in which we use it with reference to buses and trains. Christ is the destination towards which the law has all along been pointing, the ultimate justification for its existence, the full and final expression of its meaning. If they had been truly seated on board, the Jews would have recognized the terminus when it came into view. But they did not – and so reveal that they have not been travelling on the bus at all. Instead, they have been seeking 'to establish their own' righteousness (v. 3b).

What Paul means by this is illuminated by his reference to 'works' in 9:32. Israel thought the law should be fulfilled by 'works', that is, by careful attention to circumcision, observance of the Sabbath and festivals, food laws, and all the other things which marked her out as the elect people of God. These were the requirements which framed the life-style within which God's people could enjoy the covenant blessings. The atmosphere of this is well illustrated by a famous Rabbinic saying that 'Abraham sits at the entrance to Gehenna (hell) turning back the circumcised from entering'. Once circumcised, the saying implies, the blackest sinner will ultimately be delivered from hell.

But Israel had not grasped the reason for all these ethnic boundary-markers. They were not an end in themselves, but part of God's plan to bestow his righteousness upon mankind. If Israel had been attuned to that righteousness, she would have recognized it in Jesus, who is the law's 'end'.

By this statement in verse 4, Paul is not denying that the law was the way of righteousness for those Old Testament saints who turned to it out of deep reverence and love for God, and embraced it because it was his precious will for them. Psalm 119 is a celebration of delight in God's law, and rings with true godliness and devotion. Paul is denying, however, that such a saint would have remained aloof from Christ, once having seen him. The author of Psalm 119, if he had set eyes on Jesus, would have found in him all the delight he had previously found in the written law – and more.

Paul thus binds Jesus and the law closely together in this passage. His opponents felt that he drove a wedge between them, forcing his converts to choose between the law and Christ. But his reply was simply that, if we have Jesus, we have the law as well, for he is not an extra, added on top of the law, but the whole Old Testament is bound up in him. This amazing assertion leads us straight into 10:5–13, where he tackles the second, even more difficult question, 'How can the law require us to have faith in Jesus?'

The righteousness of God
In fact 'righteousness' here has a double meaning, I believe.

The Greek of verse 3a simply says, 'being ignorant of the righteousness of God'. NIV has interpreted this by putting in the phrase 'that comes from'. Was this addition justified? Although Paul uses the expression 'righteousness from God' in Philippians 3:9, where he thinks of 'righteousness' as God's gift to us, the answer is probably 'No'. He seems to have other ideas in mind here.

First, the thought of God's righteousness as expressed in the law is clearly important here. The link between verses 2 and 3 (including 'for') shows that Israel's 'zeal not based on "insight" ' is equivalent to 'being ignorant of God's righteousness': and of course her zeal was directed towards the law. The Old Testament certainly pictures the law as an expression of God's character. Its whole purpose was to enable his people to 'Be holy because I, the Lord your God, am holy' (Lv. 19:2).

Secondly, God's righteousness is often thought of in the Old Testament as that quality in him which impels him to reach out towards his rebellious creation in mercy and salvation, reclaiming man for himself and reasserting his 'right' over the world. It is a mistake to think of his righteousness simply as his righteous character, for then passages like Psalm 143:1–2 become impossible to understand:

> *O Lord, hear my prayer, listen to my cry for mercy; in your faithfulness and righteousness come to my relief. Do not bring your servant into judgment, for no-one living is righteous before you.*

Although he is aware that no-one is righteous before God, the psalmist directs his appeal for mercy precisely to the Lord's righteousness. One might have thought that God's righteousness would be the opposite of his mercy as far as sinners were concerned: his righteousness condemning us, his mercy forgiving us. But rather, his righteousness is precisely that in which sinners may place their confidence for acceptance. 'The Lord's love is with those who fear him, and his righteousness with their children's children' (Ps. 103:17). Because he is righteous, he will step in to deliver those who cannot save themselves – and salvation of course means being made acceptable in his sight, being made to bear the image of his own holiness and righteousness.

This second meaning of 'righteousness' brings to life many other New Testament passages as well. A good example is 1 John 1:9, a famous verse often used in services of worship to convey an assurance of forgiveness: 'If we confess our sins, he is faithful and just and will forgive us our sins and purify us from all unrighteousness.' His righteousness leads him to forgive.

So here in Romans 10:3–4, we can see how Israel's ignorance of God's righteousness was not just a failure truly to know him, but also a failure to understand his way of salvation. If she had approached the law with faith, she would have recognized Jesus as 'the righteousness of God' in both senses. For he reveals the wonderful righteousness of God's character both in its inner perfection, and as he stretches out his arm to rescue his world.

The right interpretation?

In all fairness it must be confessed that the interpretation of Romans 10:3–4 which has been offered in this chapter is by no means universally accepted by the commentators and other scholars. One of Britain's most respected New Testament scholars, Professor C. F. D. Moule, writes of 10:4 that it is 'one of the most hotly debated passages in the Pauline epistles'. Space will not allow a full survey and discussion of all the hot debates, but I ought at any rate to record that all is not as straightforward as the presentation above suggests. Faced with a passage like this, all I can do is to propose the interpretation which seems to me (a) to relate most clearly to the situation Paul was facing, (b) to fit in best with the overall sweep of his argument, and (c) to make the most natural sense of the language he actually uses.

Debate particularly surrounds the meaning of 'the righteousness of God' (does it really have the double meaning I have suggested here? and is the NIV really wrong to insert 'from'?), the meaning of 'end' in 10:4 (some scholars argue that it does mean 'termination', and find here a radical rejection of the law or parts of it), and the meaning of 'law' (Professor Moule in fact believes that 'law' should be translated 'legalism': Christ puts an end to legalism, that is, to the self-seeking attempt to establish one's own righteousness before God).

All in all it is one of those passages about which it will always be rash to claim that one has found the right answer, because it will always transcend our capacity to penetrate its profundity. Like the whole of Romans, therefore, it is the sort of passage to which we should keep returning, because our understanding of it ought to keep developing.

CHAPTER NINE

Fulfilling the law by faith

> [5]*Moses describes in this way the righteousness that is by the law: 'The man who does these things will live by them.' *[6]*But the righteousness that is by faith says: 'Do not say in your heart, "Who will ascend into heaven?" ' (that is, to bring Christ down), *[7]*or "Who will descend into the deep?" ' (that is, to bring Christ up from the dead). *[8]*But what does it say? 'The word is near you; it is in your mouth and in your heart,' that is, the word of faith we are proclaiming: *[9]*That if you confess with your mouth, 'Jesus is Lord,' and believe in your heart that God raised him from the dead, you will be saved. *[10]*For it is with your heart that you believe and are justified, and it is with your mouth that you confess and are saved. *[11]*As the Scripture says, 'Anyone who trusts in him will never be put to shame.' *[12]*For there is no difference between Jew and Gentile – the same Lord is Lord of all and richly blesses all who call on him, *[13]*for, 'Everyone who calls on the name of the Lord will be saved.'* (Romans 10:5–13)

These verses are very difficult to interpret. Not surprisingly, the commentators display an enormous variety of opinions. But a difficulty of this sort is something positive, not something to be regretted. For the very process of wrestling with a text like this is an education in itself, even if we may not be sure that we have discovered the whole truth!

The critics try to put the knife in

This section has called forth some sharply worded criticism of Paul. Verses 6–8 are an extended quotation of Deuteronomy 30:12–14, and some feel that the way in which he treats this text undermines his whole attempt to ground his argument in the Old Testament. 'Purely fanciful' (C. H. Dodd) . . . 'this drastic and unwarrantable allegorising must have exposed him to attack' (K. E. Kirk) . . . 'corrects the text of Moses with a supremely arbitrary hand' (H. Windisch): these are just some of the accolades he receives.

The trouble is that Paul seems to reverse the meaning of the passage he quotes. The text actually runs,

> *Now what I am commanding you today is not too difficult for you or beyond your reach. . . . No, the word is very near you; it is in your mouth and in your heart so that you may obey it.* (Dt. 30:11, 14)

There is a double problem here. Firstly, the passage is referring to obedience to the law, and is an encouragement to Israel to feel that the obedience God desires is well within her grasp. But Paul did not believe this. He denied that man is capable of obeying the law, and says so in Romans in no uncertain terms. 'Jews and Gentiles alike are all under sin . . . no-one will be declared righteous in his sight by observing the law' (Rom. 3:9, 20). Indeed, he has just roundly criticized Israel for trying to catch the law 'by works' (9:32). Secondly, Paul applies the quotation not to the law, but to 'the word of faith we are proclaiming' (v. 8). A passage which originally taught (apparently) the exact opposite is used to support salvation by faith, not works.

It is not surprising to find some scholars saying that, left to himself, Paul would have avoided this passage like the plague; but he had to say something about it because he knew his opponents would quote it back at him. So rather than beat about the bush he boldly reinterprets it to support his side of the argument. Professor A. T. Hanson describes Paul's reasoning like this: 'Once grant that . . . Deut. 30:12–14 was intended to encourage observance of the Torah, and Paul's whole case has collapsed.'

Many scholars, then, regard this section as a piece of unsuccessful rear-guard action against possible counter-arguments.

We find the same problem in verse 5, where Paul quotes another verse (Lv. 18:5) which likewise seems to support a way of salvation which he felt was impossible: 'The man who does these things [i.e. the commandments] will live by them.' There is no unspoken qualification here, like 'But of course, as we all know, no-one is in fact able to do them'. Leviticus 18:1–5 is a call to distinctiveness allied to a promise: 'Don't be like the nations around you: live the way I tell you, and you will live indeed!' Without question, this passage presupposes the capacity of man to obey the law.

Paul's critics have not yet finished. Looking ahead to verses 11–13, they note how Paul tries to justify his proclamation of the gospel to the Gentiles by quoting two more passages, Isaiah 28:16 (already quoted in 9:33), and Joel 2:32. But, they say, neither of these passages refers to the Gentiles originally, so that once again Paul has misquoted in order to support his argument.

But Paul is wearing a mail vest!

I believe there is very little truth in these accusations. Once again the real profundity of Paul's teaching has been missed. In fact his purpose is much more positive than merely forestalling an objection. The clue is given – once again – by a word which the NIV has seen fit to omit altogether. Verse 5 in fact begins in the Greek with 'For. . .'. This time, the 'for' introduces the whole paragraph, so that we can think of verses 5–13 as Paul's justification and explanation of verse 4.

With this thought in mind, we immediately notice how the words in verse 4 reappear in this section: 'believe/faith' (same root in Greek: see vv. 6, 8, 9, 10, 11); 'everyone' (see vv. 11, 12, 13); 'righteousness' (see vv. 5, 6, 10); 'Christ' (see vv. 6, 7, 9); 'the law' (see v. 5, and remember that this expression was used to refer to the Old Testament in general, and not just to the books of Moses). Only the word 'end' does not reappear, but perhaps this is because that word focuses what Paul wants to prove in the section as a whole: he wants to show that the law itself hails Christ as its end, the full and final expression of its righteousness and the achiever of its purpose. The texts which he chooses to prove this, far from being twisted and misapplied, are treated sensitively and with full appreciation of their meaning.

Saying 'yes' to Leviticus . . .

It may well be true that Paul has his opponents in mind as he quotes Leviticus 18:5 in verse 5. It is just the sort of verse to which they would turn in order to justify the continuing validity and power of God's law. What had God done or said, they would argue, to nullify this offer of life through obedience? Theirs was a powerful, water-tight argument, carrying weight just by the force of its inner coherence.

Some commentators suggest that Paul is not formally quoting in verse 5, but is simply using the language of Leviticus 18:5 to put into words the way of salvation he rejects – the way of works-righteousness. (Similarly, they say, he then goes on in verses 6–8 to use the language of Deuteronomy 30:12–14 to put into words the right way – the way of faith-righteousness.) But this does not make sense. He would be playing right into his opponents' hands if he were thus absent-mindedly to remind them of verses which so beautifully support their case and refute his. And he so kindly reminds them of the mighty authority against whom he is pitting himself, the great Moses himself.

It is much better to understand verse 5 as a genuine acknowledgment of the basic rightness of his opponents' viewpoint. He cannot simply say, 'Moses was wrong!' That would confirm their worst fears about him. If the law says it, it must be true – Paul shares this basic presupposition with his opponents. If we were right in our interpretation of Romans 9:32, Paul has already made clear his agreement that the law was not a hoax. 'Doing' the law was a real way of salvation. Similarly, he does not have his tongue in his cheek when he writes in Romans 2:18–20 that the man who has and lives by

God's law is 'a guide for the blind, a light for those who are in the dark, an instructor of the foolish . . .', because the law is 'the embodiment of knowledge and truth' (2:19f.). In 7:10 he talks about 'the very commandment that was intended to bring life . . .', and in all probability is alluding to Leviticus 18:5 there, too.

. . . *in the light of Deuteronomy*

So Paul disarms his opponents by agreeing with their basic position. But when we get to verse 6, the sting in the tail appears! It is extraordinary that Paul has so often been accused of taking texts out of context, and, more than anywhere else, precisely in this passage. But actually he is concerned here to do exactly the opposite – to interpret one part of the law in the light of another, in fact to let Deuteronomy 30:12–14 tell us how we should interpret the Lord's warm invitation and promise in Leviticus 18:5.

The 'But . . .' at the start of verse 6 gives us the clue. Paul takes us to Deuteronomy 30:12–14 in order to qualify the teaching of Leviticus 18:5, just as in Romans 9:25–29 he took us to Isaiah 10 in order to qualify the preceding quotation of Hosea. The promise of 'life' in Leviticus 18:5 does not depend solely on preserving the 'works', the distinctive marks and life-style which distinguish the Jew from the Gentile (see above, p. 93). Rather, Deuteronomy 30 summons him to a faith-righteousness, a tranformation of heart, an inner obedience. This is the 'doing' of the law which leads to life, not a constant striving to maintain the super-purity of a distinctive Judaism.

Paul probably has in mind this intense search of the Pharisees for moral and ritual perfection when he quotes the questions, 'Who will ascend into heaven? . . . Who will descend into the deep?' He grew up in Jerusalem, receiving his education from some of the greatest Pharisees of the day, and so he had imbibed from his youth their urgent striving towards an ever more detailed obedience to the law. They had built up huge bodies of case-law, to prescribe how the law should be obeyed in many different situations; and they 'fenced' the law around by many supplementary regulations, to protect themselves and their followers from ever coming near the possibility of disobedience. Many were inspired by their 'zeal for God' to undertake similar devotion. But . . .

But Paul had come to see it as essentially hopeless. In this urgent seeking for ever-purer obedience he discerned a failure to hear the encouragement of Deuteronomy 30. It is worth quoting verses 11–14 in full:

> *Now what I am commanding you today is not too difficult for you or beyond your reach. It is not up in heaven, so that you have to ask, 'Who will ascend into heaven to get it and proclaim it to us so that we may obey it?' Nor is it beyond the sea, so that you have to ask, 'Who will cross the sea to get it and proclaim it to us so that we may obey it?' No, the word is very near you; it is in your mouth and in your heart so that you may obey it.*

Properly understood, the task of obeying God is well within the reach of his people. Professor Barnabas Lindars, more sensitive than many commentators on this passage, writes about Paul's quotation of it that 'obedience from the heart will alone secure the blessing . . . For Paul the passage must be concerned with Christ, . . . for the conduct which it inculcates is precisely the attitude of faith.'

This is exactly right. 'Righteousness by faith' is all to do with the re-orientation of the heart towards God, with a new love for him expressed in glad obedience. Paul wants to show that this is not new, but is the foundation of Old Testament righteousness, as well. His ministry was aimed at bringing about 'the obedience of faith' among the Gentiles (Rom. 1:5; 16:26). By his quotation of Deuteronomy here, Paul reveals something of what he means by 'the obedience of faith'. For him, the two ideas go hand-in-hand, for faith in Christ is the writing of the law on our hearts – is he not 'the righteousness of God' in person? So the one who believes in Jesus, who confesses from the heart that 'Jesus is Lord' (v. 9), shows by that very act that the heart-obedience of Deuteronomy 30:11–14 has become a reality for him. This is a dramatic, brilliant step in Paul's argument, and one which lies at the heart of his answer to the problem of Israel.

In fact, Deuteronomy 30:11–14 marks something of a climax within the message of Deuteronomy, for earlier sections are distinctly depressing. Israel's rebellion is constantly emphasized, her hardness of heart and unwillingness to respond to the Lord. The people are 'stiff-necked' (Dt. 9:6), and need to 'circumcise the foreskin' of their heart (10:16, AV). Moses sets before them the blessing and the curse: '. . . the blessing if you obey the commands of the Lord your God . . . ; the curse if you disobey . . .' (11:26–28), and then the blessings and curses, especially the latter, are specified in great detail in chapter 28. Sadly, Moses knows that the curses will fall upon Israel, because 'to this day the Lord has not given you a mind that understands or eyes that see or ears that hear' (29:4). The second half of chapter 29 is a sad description of her future state. 'The whole land will be a burning waste of salt and sulphur . . . because this people abandoned the covenant of the Lord, the God of their fathers' (29:23, 25).

Heart-transplant

Against this background chapter 30 is much more encouraging. Through the experience of the curses the people will come to their senses, and 'the Lord your God will circumcise your hearts and the hearts of your descendants, so that you may love him with all your heart and with all your soul, and live' (Dt. 30:6). The people will be restored to the prosperity which God had all along planned for them. And then come the verses Paul quotes. They are not part of the vision of restoration which they follow, but they look back over the whole message of Deuteronomy. If only they will listen properly to the Lord, the people will realize that this whole experience of cursing and restoration is unnecessary, for obedience is within their grasp.

But we know well what their heart is like, and so the natural home of 30:12–14 is in the context of that circumcision of heart and new love for God which will characterize the nation restored after judgment.

103

This theme of the need for a transformation of heart, if the people are to love and obey God as they should, is important later in the Old Testament, especially in Jeremiah and Ezekiel. They both locate the core of Israel's problem in her hard and unrepentant heart, which constantly leads her into rebellion (*e.g.* Je. 5:23f.; 7:23f.; 17:9; Ezk. 2:3; 3:7; *etc.*), and then they both look forward to a transformation of her heart as the centre-piece of God's saving activity (Je. 31:31–33; Ezk. 11:19f.; 36:26f.). Their prophecy is vital for a right understanding of Paul's use of Deuteronomy 30, for he is claiming that it has been fulfilled in Jesus, in whom the problem of the unrepentant heart has been finally solved.

Paul has already dropped hints in this direction in Romans, for instance in 5:5 ('God's love has been poured into our hearts through the Holy Spirit', RSV), in 6:17 ('You . . . have become obedient from the heart . . .', RSV), and in 8:10 ('If Christ is in you . . . your spirit is alive'). Following his description of the corruption of heart and mind which has ruined the world (Rom. 1:18ff.), Paul shows how the renewal of the heart is at the centre of the experience of 'justification by faith'.

Applying the law to Christ

Paul does not quote Deuteronomy 'straight', in the way we quoted it above. He puts in little interpretative asides – 'that is, to bring Christ down . . . that is, to bring Christ up from the dead . . . that is, the word of faith we are proclaiming' (vv. 6, 7, 8). This is what incenses the commentators, who feel that Paul is illegitimately applying the law to Christ, claiming that he alone is able to reveal that Moses was talking about believing in Jesus rather than about obeying the law. But Paul could not possibly convince his opponents by a trick like that.

Rather, he is trying to show them that their devotion to the law is quite unnecessary, now that Christ has come. It is important to remember that his opponents were Christians. The question, 'Who will ascend into heaven?' is asked by someone who feels that obedience is beyond him, so that he needs heavenly aid. Such a question, says Paul, is actually to ask for the Messiah to come ('that is, to bring Christ down') – but in fact he has! Similarly, the force of the question 'Who will descend into the deep?' is to ask for supernatural aid against the powers of darkness which frustrate obedience. But the import of such a question is 'to bring Christ up from the dead' – which is what he has already done! The risen Christ is clearly victorious over the powers of darkness. His incarnation, death and resurrection have made such prayers redundant. The Pharisee need strive no more.

Verse 8 then turns to the positive. Paul reveals the reason underlying the asides about Christ in verses 6–7: the gospel, 'the word of faith which we preach', means that people's mouths and hearts are filled with the very 'word' which Israel, in her zeal, has been striving to fulfil. For Jesus is the 'end' of the law, and those who confess him are thereby enabled to enter the 'life' of the law itself, circumcised in heart and mind.

Paul is probably reminding his readers of their baptismal confession in verses 9 and 10, a confession that they had all made, whatever shade of theological opinion they represented. The very fact of having been brought to baptism means that they have entered into a new sphere of experience which transcends Leviticus 18:5, an experience which the Old Testament itself longs for and predicts. Their baptism into Christ was an entering into all that the law held out before them as the blessings of obedience.

Faith open to everyone!

In verses 11–13, Paul returns without hesitation to the subject so close to his heart: the inclusion of the Gentiles. For he has just given us the Old Testament justification for his Gentile ministry. This fulfilment of the law through Christ is open to all, because Christ is available for all.

He repeats his quotation of Isaiah 28:16, previously quoted in 9:33b, thus rounding the argument off and balancing 'the law' (Leviticus, Deuteronomy) with 'the prophets'. Such a balance was often required in scriptural argument. Scripture in all its parts identifies faith as the vital principle at the heart of the experience of salvation. Isaiah offered a sure foundation and security for those who would simply trust in the 'precious cornerstone' laid by the Lord in Zion.

Typically, Paul slips a subtle change into his repeat of the quotation. Instead of simply 'the one who trusts . . .', he writes 'Everyone who calls. . .'. Not a big change, one might think, and certainly not one that substantially distorts Isaiah (he too was thrilled by the thought of the in-gathering of the Gentiles to enjoy the blessings of God's people, and often writes of it). But for Paul a great deal hung on that 'everyone'. There was a vital 'everyone' in verse 4, and we must never forget the passion with which Paul believed in his call to be an apostle to the Gentiles.

He was convinced that, once faith was made the ground of salvation, then the doors had to be flung open. Faith entailed no ritual, no application forms were needed, no exams had to be taken or proofs of pedigree produced; the most unlikely people could come in on the same terms as the greatest. Hence his triumphant 'there is no difference between Jew and Gentile' (v. 12). Actually, the NIV has made this a little more shocking than in fact it is: 'distinction' would be a better translation than 'difference'. Paul was quite prepared to recognize differences between Jews and Gentiles, but he would not allow the Jews to exalt the differences into distinctions of rank or privilege before God. Jews and Gentiles stand on the same ground.

'Hear, O Israel, the Lord our God, the Lord is one'

This equality arises for Paul out of the oneness of God. If God is one and undivided, then his mind must be undivided towards his creation. Whatever the election of Israel means, therefore, it cannot mean an ultimate distinction of class or quality between Jews and Gentiles. The sub-heading above is a quotation of the Shema (Hebrew for 'hear'), the prayer which Jews still recite daily, in obedience to the command in Deuteronomy 6:4–9. As a child Paul would have heard the Shema over and over again, and his fertile and sensitive mind detected in it an overtone which his Jewish-Christian opponents had failed to see, diligent though they doubtless were in reciting it themselves. He asks pointedly in Romans 3:29f.:

> *Is God the God of Jews only? Is he not the God of Gentiles too? Yes, of Gentiles too, since there is only one God, who will justify the circumcised by faith and the uncircumcised through that same faith.*

If God is one, the human race must be one before him, and so must be his purposes of salvation. The language of the Shema probably underlies Romans 10:12 too. God is 'the same Lord' as far as all men are concerned, and all we need do is 'call on him' (v. 13).

To 'call on the name of the Lord' is a biblical expression for understanding worship and obedient submission. Paul concludes this section with a quotation of Joel 2:32 in which this idea is contained. This verse comes from the passage which Peter quotes at length on the Day of Pentecost (Acts 2:17–21), and thus is excellently suited to Paul's purpose. Here is a verse closely associated with the outpouring of the Holy Spirit on 'all people', foreshadowed in the blessing at Pentecost.

As we noted above, some commentators regard this as a misquotation too, for in its original setting in Joel, it is not certain that it concerns the Gentiles. However it does no violence to Joel to take it in this way, and a number of Old Testament scholars are quite prepared to support Paul's application of it to the Gentiles. It is clear from this passage and from the use of Joel in Acts 2 that the early church was united in this particular interpretation.

The restoration of . . . Israel?

In any case, Paul probably does not want to overthrow the primary application of this Joel passage to Israel. It has something in common with Deuteronomy 30:12–14 which we must not overlook: in their original contexts, both passages refer to a restoration of Israel after judgment, like the verses quoted in Romans 9:25–29. We looked at Paul's quotation of Deuteronomy 30 purely from an individual perspective, with reference to the new heart-obedience bestowed by Christ. But Hosea, Isaiah, Moses and Joel all think beyond merely the individual in the passages Paul quotes, and envisage a restoration of Israel corporately, through and after the judgment she inevitably incurs for her rebellion. This must be part of Paul's intention as he quotes them. As we move into Romans 11, we will discover what kind of restoration he has in mind.

In the meantime, he remains with the 'everyone' theme, as he further defends the ministry which was so dear to him, and explores in even greater depth the relationship between Jews and Gentiles in God's purposes.

CHAPTER TEN

Beautiful feet

14How, then, can they call on the one they have not believed in? And how can they believe in the one of whom they have not heard? And how can they hear without someone preaching to them? 15And how can they preach unless they are sent? As it is written, 'How beautiful are the feet of those who bring good news!'

16But not all the Israelites accepted the good news. For Isaiah says, 'Lord, who has believed our message?' 17Consequently, faith comes from hearing the message, and the message is heard through the word of Christ. (Romans 10:14–17)

Benjamin Jowett called this passage 'one of the most obscure portions of the Epistle'. The trouble is that Paul almost drops into a kind of note-form here, and it is particularly difficult to trace the linking ideas. But all is not lost.

I believe that there are two 'keys' to unlocking this passage, one theological and the other structural. The theological key is found in the last section, in which Paul almost made the law and the gospel identical, by his staggering 'that is, the word of faith we are proclaiming' in verse 8. Paul united Old and New Testaments by saying that the law's vision of the word of God written in the heart has been fulfilled in the gospel. The law all along sought to be fulfilled by faith, and now that faith has come through Jesus. This inner unity of law and gospel is a theological compass which helps us chart our course through the rest of chapter 10.

The structural key is the observation that the whole of this section of Romans, 9:30 – 10:21, is 'chiastic'. A 'chiastic' structure can be illustrated by a model railway exhibition in which the layout is on one long table around which visitors circulate. They go all down one side, looking at the trains running through the model villages and countryside, and then come back down the other side, looking at the same scene but from a different perspective, and seeing it all in a new way as a result. Bible authors in both Testaments sometimes use a similar technique in writing. They take us along a particular track to a destination, then reverse and come back to where they started, showing us everything again, but from a new angle and in reverse order. In literary terminology, a passage like this is called a 'chiasmus'.

We noticed earlier (p. 84) how 9:30 – 10:21 begins and ends with the contrast between the unexpected blessing of the Gentiles and the exclusion of rebellious Israel. That marks the beginning and end of the chiasmus – Paul ends up at the point he started from. In fact, we are now at its mid-point: In 10:14–21, Paul takes us back over the ground he has traversed since 9:30, presenting it from a different angle (and, in effect, drawing conclusions from it). (See diagram on opposite page.)

The chiasmus in 9:30 – 10:21 was probably not a deliberate construction on Paul's part. By observing it, we are simply tracing the way in which thoughts connected themselves in his mind. As a literary artist, Paul often created an 'inclusio', which is the technical name for a section which ends as it began, like Romans 9:30 – 10:21. But probably the chiastic arrangement of 10:1–17 arose spontaneously, as Paul developed his parallel between the law and the gospel.

The 'inclusio' (9:30–33 parallel to 10:18–21) forms a substantial bracket around the whole section. Within this, there is something of a new start at 10:1 ('Brothers . . .'), and something of a conclusion at 10:17 ('So then . . .'). The train of thought, rather obscurely presented with these headings, will become clearer as we move through the passage.

A		**B**
9:30–33	The blessing of the Gentiles and the failure of Israel	10:18–21
10:1–4	Rejection of the word by Jews (**A**) and Gentiles (**B**); and the vital principle of faith	10:16–17
10:5–8a	The appointed messengers: Moses, Christ (**A**), apostles (**B**) and the nearness of the word	10:15
10:8b	The preaching of the word	10:14c
10:9–11	Believing in him	10:14b
10:12–13	Calling upon the name of the Lord	10:14a

Everyone who calls on the name of the Lord will be saved

This quotation from Joel in verse 13 is the mid-point of the chiasmus, the goal towards which Paul has been leading us all along. This universal offer to Jews and Gentiles alike is the vital point that Paul wants to press home to his Jewish-Christian opponents. If the offer is applicable to all, there can be no distinction in the actual preaching of the gospel: and it is this practical implication of his gospel which Paul highlights in verse 14.

It seems likely that Paul's opponents had strong views about evangelism. Because they believed that nothing had happened to alter the uniqueness of Israel in God's plan, they probably also insisted that the gospel should be preached to Jews first. We know that there were perhaps as many as 50,000 Jews living in Rome at this time, divided into widely scattered synagogues all over the city, and we know too that the Roman church was more Gentile than Jewish in composition. Had the Jewish-Christians in the church been trying to persuade their Gentile brethren to hold back on spreading the gospel among their Gentile neighbours, and to help them in the enormous task of evangelizing the Jews? They had plenty of good theological arguments to back up their requests.

They might even have appealed to Paul's example. His missionary technique was to start preaching the gospel in the synagogue in each place, and then – usually after being thrown out! – to take the gospel to the Gentiles in a second phase of ministry (see Acts 13:45f.; 18:6; 28:23–29). Paul's friends in Rome, Priscilla and Aquila (16:3), had seen Paul adopt this pattern, when they lived with him and shared his ministry in Corinth (see Acts 18). Even if Paul's opponents were not actually saying that it was wrong in principle to evangelize Gentiles, they would certainly have been much more concerned to spread the gospel in the Roman synagogues.

Paul has himself granted that Israel has a certain priority, in Romans 1:16. But he did not say at that point exactly what he meant by 'to the Jew first, and also to the Greek' (av). Here in Romans 10, he insists that the gospel belongs in principle to all mankind, and we are reminded of his moving acknowledgment of indebtedness to all in Romans 1:14.

How can they call on him in whom they have not believed?

This is the first in a chain of four rhetorical questions (see vv. 14–15) with which Paul tackles this issue, and at the same time he begins to take us back over the ground he traversed in 10:1–13. 'They' in this first question is clearly the same as 'everyone' in verse 13: if the offer of salvation is open to all who will submit to God in reverent and intelligent worship, then clearly the invitation to believe must be issued to 'everyone'.

And how can they believe in one whom they have not heard?

The mention of 'calling upon the Lord' in verses 12–13 followed three verses in which the theme of 'faith' had been uppermost (vv. 9–11). The faith which fulfils the law is not any old faith, but is Christian faith, focusing around an intelligent ascription to Christ of the great name 'Lord', and a firm conviction of the truth of his resurrection (v. 9). If 'everyone' is to be able to take up the invitation issued in verse 13, then he must be in a position to focus his faith in this way, hearing the name of Christ and the message of the resurrection.

The NIV is wrong to insert the word 'of' here in verse 14b ('one *of* whom they have not heard'). Paul is saying that men need to hear Christ personally, if they are to come to true faith. Only such a direct encounter can bring about the transformation of heart and life which true faith entails. Paul is slowly building up his argument: the 'calling upon the Lord' which brings salvation is not any religious awareness or commitment, but is faith in a Christ who has been personally heard.

And how can they hear without a preacher?

This looks back to verse 8b, where Paul uses the same verb when he writes, 'that is, the word of faith which we are proclaiming'. His argument gathers force here in verse 14c. If it is true that the law, the 'word' which God told Israel was in her heart and mouth, finds its fulfilment in 'the word of faith', the Christian gospel, then those who are most loyal to the law should be the most keen to see it proclaimed to all who are entitled to hear. It must be preached.

Paul has not distinguished between Jews and Gentiles in these rhetorical questions – it would go right against the tenor of his argument to do so – but plainly the Gentiles are mainly in mind. If some Christians in Rome were challenging Paul's ministry, or even questioning the legitimacy of preaching the gospel to the Gentiles, Paul's words are very pointed indeed.

And how can they preach unless they are sent?

At first sight, this fourth question in verse 15a looks a little purposeless. But in fact it adds a great deal. The word translated 'sent' is the Greek verb with which the word 'apostle' is connected. An apostle was a 'sent one', and the sending implied full authority to act and speak on behalf of the sender. An apostle was more than a mere preacher: he was one with a special commission from Christ, like an Old Testament prophet who was appointed to say 'Thus says the Lord . . .', and the hearers could be sure that the Lord did indeed say it. Paul believed that, because he was an apostle, 'Christ is speaking through me' (2 Cor. 13:3) – and that is why he writes 'whom', not 'of whom', in the second question. He regarded his own ministry as being on a par with that of the Old Testament prophets. So, just as in the Old Testament God spoke to his people through chosen spokesmen, the proclamation of the gospel must be undertaken by messengers, specifically appointed by God to the task, through whom Christ himself will speak.

At the back of Paul's mind, of course, is a defence of his own apostleship to the Gentiles. In chapter 11 he will develop this defence from a more personal angle, but here he is thinking of Christian apostleship in general. The gospel cannot spread, without divine permission and divine legitimation of the mission. So (his argument runs), the very fact that the gospel has gone into all the world with such success is a proof of God's appointment of the human messengers – apostles like himself.

How beautiful . . .

Paul makes this point with a quotation from Isaiah 52:7, 'How beautiful . . . are the feet of those who bring good news!' He believed that this prophecy was being fulfilled in the gospel era: the time to which Isaiah was looking forward had now come, as gospel preachers went out with the good news of Jesus. But another vital element in Paul's use of this quotation is often overlooked. Isaiah's prophecy was being fulfilled not only by the preaching of the gospel, but also by its glad reception. When the divinely appointed messengers come, they are called 'beautiful', and their message is pronounced 'good news!'

In the chiastic structure of the chapter, verse 15 looks back to verses 5–8. Those verses too were about a message which was brought near by a divinely appointed messenger, to be welcomed into the hearts of the hearers. Moses was God's apostle to Israel, bringing the law and the offer of life through it, and urging Israel to realize that the law needed to be written on her heart. He told them not to ask the longing question, 'Who will ascend into heaven for me. . . . Who can help me achieve perfection in my obedience to God's law?', for the law had come close to them through his ministry.

But Paul now sees that such longings are a prayer for the Messiah to come. The offer of the law in the heart has been fulfilled in Jesus, who is the Apostle *par excellence*, sent to bring 'the word of faith' to us by his incarnation and resurrection. He still comes in the persons and message of his appointed apostles (10:15), for when they speak, he is heard, and when they are pronounced 'beautiful', the faith that transforms the heart is born.

So if Jesus brings the heart-obedience which the law urges its adherents to have, and if God has all along intended to save all mankind, then the universal proclamation of the gospel of Christ by his apostles is the very thing to which the law itself points. Paul's opponents cannot, therefore, oppose his ministry in the name of loyalty to the law. Such an attitude completely misunderstands the law.

But not all have obeyed the gospel

Having touched on the positive acceptance of the gospel, Paul now turns to the other side of the picture, its rejection, in verse 16. In 10:1–4, he links the failure of the Jews to believe in Christ with a failure to grasp the law: their failure to understand the law was conclusively shown by their rejection of Christ.

Now, he broadens the picture, looking at the same problem from the angle of the gospel, rather than the law. The NIV is quite wrong to insert 'the Israelites' into verse 16: Paul says simply 'not all', which plainly means 'all hearers of the gospel', both Jewish and Gentile. Including its quotation of

Isaiah 53:1 ('Lord, who has believed our message?'), verse 16 seems designed to make three points.

1. The gospel suffers exactly the same fate as the law: it meets with unbelief and rejection. The Gentiles are no better at believing the gospel than the Jews were at obeying the law. Even when Christ himself speaks through appointed apostles, the gospel meets with a mixed reception, sometimes welcomed gladly and sometimes rejected out of hand.

2. This rejection of the gospel, whether by the Jews or by the Gentiles, has not taken God by surprise. Isaiah the prophet foretold both how the gospel would be welcomed by some ('How beautiful are the feet . . .'), and rejected by others ('Who has believed. . . ?'). These two verses come virtually side by side in Isaiah, within one passage looking forward to the salvation of Israel through the Messiah. The mystery of unbelief is a constant feature of God's dealings with men. Paul has already written about this in chapter 9, with its sombre analysis of the reasons for Israel's apostasy and its location of the cause in God's mysterious purposes of election. And the same problem will occupy him throughout chapter 11.

3. The proper response to the gospel, as to the law, is obedience. Again, the NIV has obscured things somewhat by using the word 'accept' here, which is more general than the word Paul actually uses. 'They have not all obeyed the gospel' he writes (RSV), and then equates obedience with faith by adding the quotation from Isaiah 53:1. We are reminded again of 1:5 and 'the obedience of faith' which is the whole purpose of his apostleship. If the gospel means the fulfilment of the law, so that 'faith' does for people all that the law wanted to do for them, then it is easy to see how 'obedience' springs to Paul's mind as a proper description of our response to Christ.

So faith comes by hearing, and hearing through the word of Christ

Paul turns to the positive again, and – in parallel to 10:4 –

gives us a little description of the birth of true faith in verse 17. 'Consequently' shows that he is rounding off this mini-paragraph on evangelism. The faith which saves, by which the law finds its 'end', is born when an appointed messenger speaks ('hearing'), and the voice of Christ himself is heard ('the word of Christ'). Opinions differ greatly amongst the experts, but this seems to be the best interpretation. This hearing is not just receiving sound-waves into the ears. It takes place only when Christ himself is heard. For true faith to be born, there must be an encounter with the risen Christ, speaking through one of his apostles. Such an encounter does not happen automatically, whenever an apostle speaks. Both Moses and Paul, as appointed apostles, found their words falling on deaf ears. But here and there, through the words of the gospel preachers, people hear Christ himself speaking, and respond with faith and love. When that happens, true 'hearing' has taken place, a hearing that means a meeting with God and a revolution in the hearer.

CHAPTER ELEVEN

Outstretched hands

[18]*But I ask: Did they not hear? Of course they did:*

> *'Their voice has gone out into all the earth,*
> *their words to the ends of the world.'*

[19]*Again I ask: Did Israel not understand? First, Moses says,*

> *'I will make you envious by those who are not a nation;*
> *I will make you angry by a nation that has no understanding.'*

[20]*And Isaiah boldly says,*

> *'I was found by those who did not seek me;*
> *I revealed myself to those who did not ask for me.'*

[21]*But concerning Israel he says,*

> *'All day long I have held out my hands*
> *to a disobedient and obstinate people.'*

(Romans 10:18–21)

Paul rounds off this section of the letter with a string of four quotations, each of them carefully introduced so that they follow on naturally from each other. He is still

118

writing in note-form, and so makes great demands upon his readers to sense the progression of thought from one verse to the next. Because the commentators all disagree, the interpretation proposed here must simply take its place alongside other suggestions. But it seems to me to make sense.

Getting the outline clear

We have already noticed how these verses balance the beginning of the section in 9:30–33, contrasting the Gentiles, who have stumbled upon the Lord all unexpectedly, with Israel, who has fallen out of fellowship with him – again, quite contrary to expectation. When he returns to the contrast here, Paul doubles it. We can set out the pattern like this:

> Verse 18: *Gentiles*. 'But I ask: "Did . . . not. . . ?" ' Response to question: Psalm 9:4
> Verse 19: *Israel*. 'Again I ask: "Did . . . not. . . ?" ' Response to question: Deuteronomy 32:21
> Verse 20: *Gentiles*. Isaiah 65:1: God reveals himself to, and is found by, those who were not seeking him.
> Verse 21: *Israel*. Isaiah 65:2: God stretches out his hands in constant appeal to rebellious and uncooperative Israel.

Verses 18 and 19 have an identical structure, introduced by questions identically worded (NIV should not have put in 'again' in verse 19), which lead into quotations. We can also see again Paul's desire to supplement the Law with the prophets, so that his argument is supported from both of the great divisions of Scripture.

The double quotation from Isaiah 65 in verses 20–21 poses no great difficulties. But those in verses 18 and 19 are much more difficult. For this reason, it is advisable to start with verses 20–21 and work backwards:

'Isaiah is even bolder'

I am drawn to this GNB translation of Paul's introductory phrase in verse 20. The verb he uses points to a contrast between Isaiah and Moses, as though Isaiah puts even more forcefully the point that Paul has just been making from Deuteronomy 32. In fact, this shows his sensitivity, for there are close links in the Hebrew between Deuteronomy 32 and Isaiah 65 which extend far beyond the actual verses he quotes.

In essence, the point is clear, for it is the same as that in 9:30: though living in ignorance of him, the Gentiles have suddenly become the object of a special revelation of the God of Israel. This leads into verse 21, where Paul quotes two phrases from the next verse, picking up a contrast which Isaiah himself draws: unlike the Gentiles, who have gladly responded, Israel remains 'disobedient and obstinate' towards God, even though he continues to extend his hands towards her in appeal for repentance and faith.

Because these two verses round off Paul's argument, they give us the clue for understanding verses 18–19. They do so by prompting us to ask two questions. Reading verse 20, concerning the Gentiles, we ask, 'What exactly is this revelation of himself that God has given to them?' This question is answered by verse 18. Reading verse 21, concerning Israel, we ask, 'What exactly is the appeal which God makes to Israel?' This question is answered by verse 19.

With these questions in mind, we move back to verses 18–19, and discover that their teaching (especially verse 19) is absolutely vital for Paul's whole solution to the problem of Israel. In fact we meet again the 'periscope' technique which we noticed in 9:24: Paul mentions briefly something which is going to figure importantly later on. In 11:11–32 the submarine under the periscope surfaces, and so we must take care to notice it properly when it appears here.

Two competing theologies

Part of the 'periscope' concerns a further aspect of the situation in which Paul was writing. Thus far, we have only considered the Jewish-Christian position which Paul was seeking to oppose. But in fact Paul had to argue on two fronts, against a distinctive Gentile-Christian theology as well as a Jewish-Christian.

We meet this Gentile-Christian theology explicitly in 11:17–24, but it appears here too. In essence, they were arguing that the Gentile church had replaced Israel in God's plan, because the Gentiles had responded with faith where Israel had refused to believe. Their 'text' could have been the parable of the wicked husbandmen, with its punch-line, 'Therefore I tell you that the kingdom of God will be taken away from you and given to a people who will produce its fruit' (Mt. 21:43). This verse could easily be used to 'prove' that Israel has lost her position in the covenant, and God has turned decisively to the Gentiles.

This is precisely what Paul himself was accused of saying by his Jewish-Christian opponents. But he wanted nothing of it, for it did indeed mean a radical rejection of the Old Testament. If there were Christians holding both these competing theologies in the Roman church, we can easily imagine the tension there must have been. (When Paul addresses the 'weak' and the 'strong' in chapter 14, we see some of the practical ways in which this tension was manifested.) In 10:18–19, Paul fires off a salvo in both directions, against both of these competing theologies together, anticipating his argument in 11:11ff.

The word of Christ universally proclaimed

The 'But . . .' at the start of verse 18 sets the right direction: Paul is countering a thought that might arise, following verse 17. This thought is clearly related to 'hearing': he wrote in verse 17 about a limited hearing, one which only takes place when Christ himself is heard to speak (through the mouth of an appointed messenger). Such a hearing is essential, if faith is to be born. 'But . . .' the fact that this sort of 'hearing' is essential for faith does not mean that those who have not 'heard' in this way have any kind of excuse for their unbelief!

On the contrary, he argues, 'they' have indeed heard – 'they' being the subject of the preceding verses, the Gentile world which is the proper object of an evangelistic ministry.

Even if they have not responded with faith, they have still 'heard' sufficiently to render them without excuse for not believing; and even if they have not actually heard an appointed messenger, they still have before them the witness of creation to God's power and deity, which is quite sufficient to deprive them of all excuse. If Gentile Christians wish to preen themselves on their faith, let them reflect on the fact that Gentile rejection of the 'word of Christ' is just as widespread as Jewish: for the proclamation of that word has gone out 'to the ends of the world', but there has been no massive response.

We recognize the typically Pauline shape of this argument. Faith is a gift of God, yet we are to blame if we do not have it! The mystery of unbelief (v. 16) is explained by the fact that mere auditory reception of the message is not sufficient to provoke faith – there has to be a 'hearing' of Christ himself (v. 17). But when 'not all obey', we cannot conclude that Christ has not made himself universally available. Every opportunity has already been given for all men to respond appropriately to the grace and goodness of God.

Paul uses Psalm 19:4 to express this, for it nicely combines the two thoughts of the human proclamation, and the witness of creation. We are reminded of Romans 1:19–20, where likewise he taught that the witness of creation renders man 'without excuse'. His claim is bold indeed: Christian missionary activity matches the 'word' addressed by creation to the conscience of mankind. There is never an excuse for unbelief.

The commentators almost unanimously feel that Paul uses Psalm 19:4 just to refer to the geographical spread of Christian missionary activity in his day. Just as Psalm 19:4 pictures the all-pervasive light of the heavenly bodies, so (this interpretation runs) Christian missionaries have brought the light of the gospel into every dark corner.

But this was simply not true – and both Paul and his readers knew it. He himself, at the time of writing Romans, was projecting a missionary trip to Spain (Rom. 15:20–24). How could he honestly base his argument here on the universal spread of Christian missionary preaching?

This objection is forceful, but not fatal. For Paul says similar things elsewhere. In Colossians 1:6 he writes, 'All over the world this gospel is producing fruit and growing, just as it has been doing among you . . .', and he greets the Corinthians '. . . together with all those in every place who call on the name of our Lord Jesus Christ' (1 Cor. 1:2). In both cases the same geographical objection could be made.

Paul may simply be using exaggerated language, but there are indications that there is more to it than this. In 1 Timothy 3:16 he quotes from a fascinating little hymn which helps us here. Jesus, says the hymn, 'was manifested in the flesh, vindicated in the Spirit, seen by angels, preached among the nations, believed on in the world, taken up in glory' (RSV).

This is a summary of Jesus' career. But the ascension comes last, following the universal proclamation of the gospel and a universal response. Historically, the conversion of the world takes place in the interval between the ascension of Christ and his return in glory (and that is how Paul views it in 1 Cor. 15:22–28). But theologically, Christ returned to glory bringing with him a redeemed world, a Victor with the spoils of war in his train – and this is the thought in 1 Timothy 3:16 (as also in Eph. 2:6 and 4:8–10).

So it would not be impossible for Paul to think of the gospel as having already embraced the whole world. The imagery of ·Psalm 19:4 fits this beautifully. As the great lights of heaven embrace and illumine the world, so does the gospel of Christ, who has already reconciled it to God.

But could Paul also be using the psalm in its original sense? It would be out of character for him to disregard it entirely. The fact that he has already written about the witness of creation in Romans 1, and the fact that the idea fits in so well with the train of thought here in Romans 10, suggest that it must be relevant.

For Psalm 19 is divided into two sections, the first (vv. 1–6) celebrating the revelation of God in creation, and the second (vv. 7–14) celebrating the revelation of that God as 'the Lord' in his law. The idea is clear: what creation says simply about 'God', the law says in detail about 'the Lord'! Paul believed that Christ was God's agent in creation (Col. 1:16), and he has just been at great pains to show how the gospel fulfils the law. So it would not be at all surprising if he saw a link between the witness of creation and the gospel of Christ. Whether through apostolic proclamation or through the testimony of the heavens, all men have heard the word of Christ, whatever their state of faith or unbelief.

So the actual thrust of Paul's argument in verse 18, I believe, is to oppose the viewpoint that the Gentiles have stepped into the space vacated by Israel as God's chosen people, by showing how they are just as guilty of unbelief as Israel ever was.

The Gentiles – a message to Israel, with love

Paul turns to Israel in verse 19. NIV's 'did' is misleading, for he is not speaking of a past generation, but of the present. In fact 'does' would be better. (The Greek 'aorist' tense, which occurs here, can sometimes be used in contexts where in English we would use a present.)

'Does Israel not know?' he asks, leaving us wondering *what* Israel knows! The commentators abound in suggestions. The best answer is the simplest: 'Does Israel not know that God has always intended to save the Gentiles?' This fits neatly into the flow of Paul's argument. His Jewish-Christian opponents should not have been surprised by the blessing of the Gentiles, for even as far back as Moses the word went out that such a blessing, should it ever occur, would be a vital message from the Lord to Israel: Deuteronomy 32:21.

This quotation comes from the middle of the 'Song of Witness' (Dt. 32:1–43), which Moses was instructed to teach to Israel just before his death. God told him that, after his death, the Israelites would certainly go astray and judgment would fall upon them (Dt. 31:16–18), yet even in their apostasy 'this song will testify against them, because it will not be forgotten by their descendants' (Dt. 31:21).

The Song first reminds Israel of the greatness of her God (32:1–4) and of her ungrateful rebellion (vv. 5–6), before going on to list in detail God's grace to Israel (vv. 7–14) and her frightful apostasy in response (vv. 15–18). Verses 19–27 describe the Lord's response to Israel's rebellion, including horrific judgment, verses 28–35 lament over her situation, and finally the Lord re-affirms his commitment to Israel in spite of her sin (vv. 34–43). The whole Song is important for the New Testament, for it is quoted on at least nine other occasions, and obviously exercised great influence on early Christians. Paul quotes from it again later in Romans – at 12:19 and 15:10.

Paul felt that he was living in precisely the situation in which the Song was intended to minister to Israel. And the particular verse he quotes allows him to spike the guns of both sets of opponents, by making the blessing of the Gentiles an expression of God's undying concern for Israel. By blessing the Gentiles, the Lord has imitated Israel's rebellion. She 'made me jealous by what is no god' (Dt. 32:21a), so the Lord in response decides to 'make you envious by those who are not a nation'. This 'not-a-nation' is of course the Gentiles, who once were 'no people' but are now called 'my people' (Rom. 9:25)!

In the Song, this blessing of another nation is a warning of judgment to come, and an appeal for repentance. It is not a complete rejection of Israel. Rather, the Lord is stretching out his hands to Israel precisely through his blessing of the Gentiles. It is not too late for her to heed the appeal, stimulated to jealousy by the sight of Gentiles embracing her God beyond her borders, and enjoying the righteousness which should be hers. We must recognize the dark side of this quotation, for the appeal is also a warning. If Paul had lived to experience the Jewish War, which broke out only ten years after the writing of Romans, and which resulted in the complete destruction of Jerusalem, it is quite clear how he would have interpreted it. The Song foretold it, standing like a sentinel over the whole of Israel's history.

But even so, the Song ends with a moving commitment by the Lord to deliver and heal his people. Judgment does not mark the end of his concern for Israel. So Gentile-Christians cannot argue that Israel has finally forfeited her position as

God's chosen race, nor can Jewish-Christians maintain that the law-free mission to the Gentiles is illegitimate and should be stopped. We shall see, as we move into Romans 11, how important Deuteronomy 32 is for Paul's argument.

The remnant and the rest

²⁵*I ask then: Did God reject his people? By no means! I am an Israelite myself, a descendant of Abraham, from the tribe of Benjamin. ²God did not reject his people, whom he foreknew. Don't you know what the Scripture says in the passage about Elijah – how he appealed to God against Israel: ³'Lord, they have killed your prophets and torn down your altars; I am the only one left, and they are trying to kill me'? ⁴And what was God's answer to him? 'I have reserved for myself seven thousand who have not bowed the knee to Baal.' ⁵So too, at the present time there is a remnant chosen by grace. ⁶And if by grace, then it is no longer by works; if it were, grace would no longer be grace.*

⁷What then? What Israel sought so earnestly it did not obtain, but the elect did. The others were hardened, ⁸as it is written:

> *'God gave them a spirit of stupor,*
> *eyes so that they could not see*
> *and ears so that they could not hear,*
> *to this very day.'*

⁹And David says,

> *'May their table become a snare and a trap,*
> *a stumbling-block and a retribution for them.*
> *¹⁰May their eyes be darkened so they cannot see,*
> *and their backs be bent for ever.'*

(Romans 11:1–10)

127

In Romans 11, Paul draws the threads of his argument together and presents his conclusions. We naturally fix our eyes on 11:26, '. . . and so all Israel will be saved', a vitally important verse in the discussion about the place of Israel in God's plan. Hopefully, our careful journey through Paul's whole argument will equip us to interpret 11:26 rightly.

The structure of Romans 11 is clear.

> *11:1–10, present.* Paul uses a further selection of texts to summarize his argument so far, in order to explain Israel's present state before God.
>
> *11:11–32, future.* As Paul looks ahead, he focuses on two things:
> Verses 11–24 pick up the picture of judgment in 11:1–10: what attitude should Gentile Christians adopt towards Israel in her apostasy?
> Verses 25–32 pick up the promise of salvation in 11:1–10: how will God ultimately fulfil his plan for Israel?
>
> *11:33–36, praises.* Having concluded his argument, Paul's heart sings with adoration.

In 11:1, Paul re-poses the question underlying his whole discussion. Has God rejected his people? The very verses Paul has just quoted in 10:20–21 could be taken to teach this. But once again, he rejects the suggestion energetically. However depressing 10:21 may be, with its picture of God vainly appealing to rebellious Israel, we cannot conclude that he has given up his appeal and turned to the Gentiles instead. In these verses, Paul looks back over Romans 9 – 10 and summarizes what he has already said about the problem of Israel, supporting his argument further by using a different set of scriptures.

Look at me!

He points to himself to disprove the view that God has rejected his people. Paul could be using his own case just as one example of a Jew who has become a Christian; or perhaps he thinks of himself as special. We remember Moses, whose acceptance into God's presence in Exodus 33:18 – 34:7 was a pledge from God that he would not destroy Israel after the golden calf episode. Did Paul think of his own conversion likewise as a kind of pledge that others would follow? (He says something like this in 1 Timothy 1:16). Either way, he is making the point that God turned Saul the persecutor into Paul the apostle, not out of a passing whim, but in fulfilment of his promises to Abraham. It is as Abraham's 'seed' – that vital word again – that Paul has been brought to know his Messiah.

Look at 1 Samuel 12!

In his denial in verse 2, 'God did not reject his people', Paul deliberately uses the language of 1 Samuel 12:22. To suggest that God has rejected Israel is to deny the clear teaching of this verse. For the Lord gave this promise in a similar situation: Israel rebelled against him, and (as they confessed) 'added to all our other sins the evil of asking for a king' (1 Sa. 12:19), instead of trusting the Lord to deliver them. Samuel warns them of judgment to come, but assures them at the same time that they are not rejected, 'because the Lord was pleased to make you his own' (1 Sa. 12:22b). His election transcends their rebellion. The phrase 'whom he foreknew', which Paul has added to his quotation, gives the reason for this assurance. Whatever her sin, Israel is still foreknown, elect, special.

Look at Elijah!

In verses 2–4 Paul turns to an even deeper period of apostasy in Israel's history – in the time of Elijah. In his situation, Samuel felt impelled as a prophet to pray *for* Israel in her sin (1 Sa. 12:23): but things were so bad for Elijah that he felt he had to pray *against* her (v. 2). He believed that he was the only Israelite who had remained faithful (v. 3, quoting 1 Ki.

19:10, 14), and there was a danger that even his witness would be extinguished. But God's reply revealed that he had not let things slide that much. Though things looked so grim, he was still fulfilling his plan for Israel, in that 'seven thousand men' – a perfect number, speaking of the complete fulfilment of God's will – 'have not bowed the knee to Baal'.

Paul is not really drawing a personal parallel between himself and Elijah, although he too was persecuted for his life by hostile Jews. It is their situations which are the same. If God was still sovereign over his chosen people in Elijah's day, even when they seemed to have turned their backs on him completely, then the same must be true following the Jews' rejection of Christ. And Paul feels that God's rule over his people is expressed in the same way, by the preserving of a 'remnant' who, like himself, embodies what it means to be a true 'Israelite'. Verse 5 draws the parallel: 'So too, at the present time there is a remnant chosen by grace.'

We remember the conclusion of his argument in 9:6–29, where the idea of the 'remnant' first appeared. Judgment for sin is inevitable – in fact, it comes to Israel within the covenant, not in violation of it. But at the heart of judgment there will always be a purpose of mercy, a 'seed', a re-'calling', a remnant in whom the promises are fulfilled (9:25–29).

Man at work – or God at work?

Paul adds verse 6 to guard against a misunderstanding. In both his time and Elijah's, the remnant exists 'by grace'. Resisting the temptation to worship Baal was not a 'work' performed by the seven thousand, on which the fulfilment of God's plan for Israel depended. If it had been so, his plan would really have been in jeopardy: what if they had not resisted? Rather, their faithfulness was the result of his 'grace', and so showed his determination that his plan will not be overturned by the sin of man. Similarly, Jewish Christians find themselves joined to the Messiah not because of their adherence to the law, but solely because God has determined to bless them.

In 9:30 – 10:21 Paul's argument rested on the simple, undeniable fact that the Gentiles have indeed come to enjoy the righteousness of God in Christ, and Paul was seeking to understand this scripturally. Here in 11:5–6 he summarizes the fact and relates it to Israel. God has not rejected his people. He is still acting for them, but *he* is acting, not *they*! His blessing of the Gentiles by 'grace', apart from 'works of the law', contains a lesson for Israel. He wants to deal with her in the same way, 'apart from the law' (3:21), creating a remnant by grace just as in the time of Elijah.

Look at Moses, Isaiah and David!

That emphasis on God's action leads us into the sad and sobering verses 7–10. For if the 'remnant', of which Paul is a conspicuous example, has been created by grace, then what of the 'rest'? If God has divided Israel by acting to create the remnant, is the unbelief of the 'rest' also his creation? Paul tackled this question boldly in Romans 9, with reference to Pharaoh and the 'vessels of wrath' (9:17–23), and he summarizes his answer here. There, he did not flinch from saying that 'God has mercy on whom he wants to have mercy, and he hardens whom he wants to harden' (9:18), although we did not understand this to mean that 'mercy' and 'hardening' are equal and opposite actions, identically attributable to him (see above, pp. 54–56). Rather, 'hardening' is a 'handing-over' (1:24, 26, 28), being left to the consequences of one's own rebellion, whereas mercy is a direct intervention to reverse the course of events.

This qualification, however, was more for our benefit than for Paul's. Like the book of Exodus, he does not shrink from making God the agent of the hardening. For if God is sovereign over his creation (9:20–21), then it must ultimately be shaped according to his will. And so here in 11:7–10 Paul likewise directly ascribes the division in Israel to God's will. He uses a passive verb in verse 7b, 'the rest were hardened', but when he supports this with an Old Testament quotation in verse 8, he uses an active verb with God as the subject: 'God gave them a spirit of stupor. . .'. The quotations that follow (from Deuteronomy, Isaiah and Psalms – from all three divisions of the Old Testament) are terrible in their picture of an Israel unresponsive, cursed and fallen – by the will of God.

Some commentators feel that Paul creates a great tension here. Having started off (11:1) with a passionate denial that God has rejected his people, they say, he ends up with quotations which seem to shout the opposite. This view of 11:1–10 is then made the basis for their exposition of 11:11–32: Paul needs to resolve the tension, which he does by predicting the reversal of this judgment and the conversion of Israel (11:26).

But Paul has said it all before. 9:6–29 started off with just such a round denial, that God's word to Israel had fallen, but we saw that his support for this included some horrifying quotations about Israel's experience of judgment, like these in 11:8–10. The point was that judgment came to Israel within the covenant, as promised. And here, with a different set of verses, Paul makes the same point: even in the present, with Israel divided by the unbelief of the 'rest', God's word and will are being fulfilled.

In fact this thought also lurks in the quotations from 1 Samuel 12 and 1 Kings 19. The assurance in 1 Samuel 12:22, 'the Lord will not reject his people', does not free Israel from judgment for her sin. On that very day, they experienced the Lord's anger at their request for a king, in a violent thunderstorm which damaged the harvest (1 Sa. 12:16–18); and Samuel assures them, immediately after telling them that God will not reject them, that 'if you persist in doing evil, both you and your king will be swept away' (1 Sa. 12:25).

This is even clearer in the case of Elijah. Paul has adapted 1 Kings 19:18 to match his own emphasis that the seven thousand were already identified and made separate 'by grace', even at the moment of Elijah's complaint. In fact the Lord uses the future tense there ('I will leave seven thousand in Israel') and the context makes it clear that this is the group who will survive the judgment which is coming upon Israel for slaying the prophets and tearing down the altars.

Paul has consciously made this adaptation. Perhaps this is why he adds verse 6, to justify importing the idea of election into the story. At no time have Israel's virtues come by any other route than 'by grace'! – because at all times God's faithfulness to his covenant promises has been expressed as much through the covenant curses as the covenant blessings. Although Paul removes a direct reference to judgment, by changing the tense of the verb from future to past, the thought of judgment is basic to his use of 1 Kings 19.

Reaching rock bottom

With the quotations in verses 8–10 we reach rock bottom, and understand Paul's grief over Israel with renewed insight. It must have torn his heart, but Paul would not let his love for Israel dictate the agenda. He was pressed by the Old Testament to see Israel as under the judgment of God, blinded by a 'spirit of stupor' from seeing him (v. 8), and as the object of a prayer that this state might continue (vv. 9–10).

Verse 8 is a complex mixture drawn from three sources. The basic quotation is of Deuteronomy 29:4, in which Moses complains that Israel simply does not have the capacity to understand and obey (and therefore will surely come under judgment): 'To this day the Lord has not given you a mind that understands or eyes that see or ears that hear.' Paul has added phrasing from two verses in Isaiah, which make it sharper, as follows:

From Isaiah 29:10 he draws the phrase 'spirit of stupor' ('The Lord has brought over you a deep sleep', NIV. 'Spirit of stupor' would actually be a better translation of the Hebrew than 'deep sleep'.) And from Isaiah 6:9 he gives the sentence its shape, turning the verb from negative to positive, so that the Lord actually gives eyes that do not see (rather than merely *not* giving eyes that *do* see).

Paul feels that the situation in his day is the same as in Isaiah's. Isaiah 6 describes the prophet's call, and the depressing commission he received. The Lord makes it clear that his ministry will deepen Israel's blindness and make judgment even more inevitable: 'Until the cities lie ruined and without inhabitant . . . until the Lord has sent everyone far away and the land is utterly forsaken' (Is. 6:11–12). A major feature of his ministry, therefore, is the announcing of judgment, such as he undertakes in the face of defeat by Assyria in Isaiah 10:20ff., the passage which Paul applies to contemporary Israel in Romans 9:27–28. There is nothing new about judgment – or about being a prophet.

Sadder still

But with the quotation of Psalm 69:22–23 Paul reaches even sadder depths in verses 9–10. This psalm is frequently applied to Jesus in the New Testament, for the sufferings of David were seen to find their fulfilment in him. From this psalm comes the verse that Jesus fulfilled on the cross, by saying 'I thirst' (Ps. 69:21; Jn. 19:28; *cf.* Mt. 27:48), and Paul quotes from it again later in Romans (15:3), where it is clear that he accepts this application to him.

He applies it to Jesus consistently. If the earlier part of the psalm describes his sufferings, and particularly his crucifixion, then the later part must apply to him too, where David prays for God's judgment upon his persecutors. From this later section of the psalm come the verses Paul quotes.

Of course, Jesus actually prayed, 'Father, forgive them, for they do not know what they are doing' (Lk. 23:34). Paul seems to envisage him praying exactly the opposite here. But the two are not inconsistent. Just as the blood of Abel cried to the Lord for vengeance (Gn. 4:10), so the blood of God's Christ is in itself an appeal for his justice and judgment, even though the Christ himself, and his apostle after him, long that it should be otherwise. So Paul carefully distances these words from Jesus himself – 'and David says. . .'. But they are messianic words nonetheless, warning of the judgment appropriate for those who have persecuted and murdered the Messiah.

Could Paul have written these words without weeping? He hears the Scriptures giving voice to a prayer that, for her rejection of the Messiah, Israel's whole lifestyle (her 'table') should poison her instead of feeding her, and lead to her downfall as a 'retribution' upon her, and that this state of blindness should continue 'for ever'. The awful reality of judgment presses in upon him – as it did upon Israel just ten years later, when the Christians fled from Jerusalem, and the Roman armies closed around the city.

CHAPTER THIRTEEN

How should Gentiles think about Israel?

[11]Again I ask: Did they stumble so as to fall beyond recovery? Not at all! Rather, because of their transgression, salvation has come to the Gentiles to make Israel envious. [12]But if their transgression means riches for the world, and their loss means riches for the Gentiles, how much greater riches will their fulness bring!

[13]I am talking to you Gentiles. Inasmuch as I am the apostle to the Gentiles, I make much of my ministry [14]in the hope that I may somehow arouse my own people to envy and save some of them. [15]For if their rejection is the reconciliation of the world, what will their acceptance be but life from the dead? If the part of the dough offered as firstfruits is holy, then the whole batch is holy; if the root is holy, so are the branches.

[17]If some of the branches have been broken off, and you, though a wild olive shoot, have been grafted in among the others and now share in the nourishing sap from the olive root, [18]do not boast over those branches. If you do, consider this: You do not support the root, but the root supports you. [19]You will say then, 'Branches were broken off so that I could be grafted in.' [20]Granted. But they were broken off because of unbelief, and you stand by faith. [21]Do not be arrogant, but be afraid. For if God did not spare the natural branches, he will not spare you either.

[22]Consider therefore the kindness and sternness of God: sternness to those who fell, but kindness to you, provided that you continue in his kindness. Otherwise, you also will

be cut off. 23And if they did not persist in unbelief, they will be grafted in, for God is able to graft them in again. 24After all, if you were cut out of an olive tree that is wild by nature, and contrary to nature were grafted into a cultivated olive tree, how much more readily will these, the natural branches, be grafted into their own olive tree! (Romans 11:11–24)

In this chapter we tackle a longer section, partly because there are fewer puzzles in it (though still plenty of difficulties), and partly because the whole section deals with one subject, summarized in the chapter-heading above. Building upon all that he has said about Israel, Paul now turns to his Gentile-Christian readers (us included), and tells us what our attitudes to Israel should be. This section therefore has very clear relevance for us today. When we compare what Paul says here with the attitudes adopted by the church down the centuries, we are put to shame as Christians.

Once again, we find that the overall flow of Paul's argument in Romans 9 – 11 affects the way in which we interpret his message here in 11:11–24.

We can divide these verses into six sub-sections, each dealing with a different aspect of the attitudes which Paul wants Gentiles to have, although there are no actual divisions in the natural progression of Paul's argument.

Longing (verses 11–12)

This is the first element in the proper Gentile attitude to Israel. Just as in 9:14, 19 (and 6:1, 15 and 7:7, 13 before that), Paul proposes a double objection to his argument in 11:1, 11, with the second objection picking up the first. So verse 11 amplifies 'Has God rejected his people?' (v. 1, RSV) in the light of verses 1–10. Relating the verses in this way reveals what Paul means by 'Have they stumbled so as to fall?' (v. 11, RSV).

For the depressing verses quoted in 11:8–10 might lead to the conclusion that 'the rest' were so far beyond hope that they could be ignored. If God has thus turned from 'the rest', a Gentile Christian might argue, and is fulfilling his commitment to Israel by saving 'the remnant', then we should follow his example, and effectively turn our backs on the unbelieving majority of Jews. This is, of course, what Christians have in fact done, for centuries. But Paul thinks otherwise. The second half of verse 11 shows that he has missionary activity in mind when he poses the question. If 'the rest' have been 'hardened' (v. 7), should we give up missionary hope for Israel, because she has 'fallen'?

No! Referring back to 10:19, Paul reminds us that his whole Gentile mission depends on Israel for its existence. Viewed from the perspective of the 'Song of Moses' (Dt. 32), it was 'because of their transgression' that he was appointed to take the gospel to the Gentiles, and so the whole Gentile expansion of the church can be seen as a message to Israel, 'to make Israel envious'. Of course, Paul has also quoted verses to show that God intended the salvation of the Gentiles anyway (Rom. 9:33; 10:13, 20). But he gives prominence to Deuteronomy 32, because it puts us Gentiles in our place. According to the 'Song', God would not have turned to the Gentiles, had he not wished to appeal to Israel by saving people right outside the covenant.

This means an attitude of longing, that the process should work. Paul expresses this longing in verse 12. Unfortunately, most of the translations (like NIV) obscure this by inserting 'will' towards the end of the verse. But Paul actually uses no verb at all, leaving us to supply the sense from the context. Because of the reference to the 'Song' and the 'jealousy' idea, it is much better to read verse 12 as an expression of longing, rather than as a prediction. So J. B. Phillips translates it: 'If their offence means the enrichment of the world, and if their falling-off means the enrichment of the Gentiles, how much more their coming to full strength!'

By putting it this way, Paul hints that it is in the Gentiles' interest to long for the salvation of Israel as he himself does. What blessing might result, if Israel responded to God's appeal!

Priority (verses 13–14)

Paul underlines his point about mission. He reveals that the whole purpose of the Gentile ministry, which brought so much criticism upon his head, was not to undermine Israel's place in God's plan, but actually to uphold it. No aspect of his apostolic ministry was unrelated to his desire to see Israel prompted into faith by envy. 'I make much of my ministry,' he says – literally 'I glorify' it. We see what he means by this in Romans 15:17–19:

> I glory in Christ Jesus in my service to God. I·will not venture to speak of anything except what Christ has accomplished through me in leading the Gentiles to obey God by what I have said and done – by the power of signs and miracles, through the power of the Spirit.

He goes on immediately to write of his plan to visit Jerusalem with the money collected in his Gentile-Christian churches for 'the poor among the saints in Jerusalem' (15:26). In the love and generosity of his converts, he wants Jews to see God's hand at work, so that the 'envy' process might be triggered. In addition, he clearly took every opportunity actually to tell Jews about God's power at work among the Gentiles through him.

So even though his activity was directed towards Gentiles, his strategy focused on Israel. This is so different from our outlook on church growth today. But Paul would encourage us to see that, wherever Gentiles turn to Christ, their faith is still an implicit appeal to Israel. Paul does not make this the sole reason for his Gentile mission, but he does emphasize it. It cannot be right, therefore, that we have completely forgotten the thought that was constantly at the back of his mind as he ministered in the pagan strongholds of Ephesus and Corinth – and Rome. We too need to ask what we should do today in order to give this 'envy' process a chance to work.

Respect (verses 15–16)

The 'for' at the start of verse 15 is vital: Paul summarizes the theological reasons for giving Israel strategic priority in Christian mission. If the Gentiles grasp these reasons, they will form a deep respect for the role Israel plays in God's plan.

Verse 15 has the same shape as verse 12, and also has no verb. Like verse 12, therefore, it is best read as an exclamation expressing deep desire. If Israel's rejection has meant the reconciliation of 'the world' to God (because of the first stage of the 'envy' process), then what would Israel's restoration mean (if the second stage operated)? But verse 15 moves beyond verse 12 in that here Paul specifies what Israel's conversion would mean for the rest of the world – 'life from the dead'.

The traditional 'Reformed' interpretation of this 'life from the dead' is that Israel's conversion will be followed by a massive, world-wide revival, almost as though the 'envy' process will have a third stage of operation, affecting the Gentiles once again. But Paul's use of the words 'reconciliation' and 'life' in Romans 5:10 points to a different interpretation: 'For if, when we were God's enemies, we were reconciled to him through the death of his Son, how much more, having been reconciled, shall we be saved through his life!'

This verse too has the same 'if . . . how much more' structure, and also concerns our present experience of 'reconciliation'. But 'life' is clearly related to the final resurrection in Christ. The same is likely to be true in 11:15: Paul is saying that Israel's restoration, should it come about, would mean 'life', resurrection, for the whole world.

His meaning becomes clearer in 11:25–26, where he picks this thought up and expands it. But the basic idea is clear: because of Israel's sin, 'the world' – that is, the Gentile world – has been brought back to God. If the other half of humanity (Israel) were also saved, then the work of salvation would be complete. What could this completion mean, he asks, but 'life from the dead' for the whole world? It could mean nothing other than the ultimate 'enrichment' of the final resurrection, the fulfilment of God's whole plan.

Paul follows this up in verse 16 by starting to give reasons why such a longing is not a blind hope. In spite of the reality of divine judgment, there are features of Israel's situation which encourage him to believe that God's plan has not been fulfilled by the present distinction between the remnant and 'the rest'. He uses two agricultural or horticultural metaphors, about which commentators disagree, but the main lines of application are clear.

The first is that of the 'first-fruits'. Paul is referring to Numbers 15:17–20, and the Old Testament custom of bringing the first-fruits of the harvest to God. By definition, the first-fruits heralded the rest of the harvest, and offering them to God was a way of thanking him for the whole. Paul invites us to think of the Jewish-Christian 'remnant' in this way – as the first-fruits of a greater harvest yet to come.

What justification can Paul give, for thinking of the 'remnant' as 'first-fruits'? In the following verses he gradually builds his case up, moving slowly from longing for Israel's restoration, to certainty that it will happen. The second picture in verse 16 begins to take him along this road: here 'the root' is probably best taken to refer to the origin of Israel in the election of the patriarchs, confirmed by all the blessings listed in 9:4–5. The tree must surely share the nature of its root, argues Paul; it must ultimately be 'holy' to the Lord. In the end, he is hinting, we may indeed expect that the 'envy' process will work.

Dependence (verses 17–18)

Paul now draws out the implication of the 'envy' process for Gentile Christians. If God has blessed us as envisaged in Deuteronomy 32, then by definition it is the blessings of Israel which have been showered upon us. Extending the 'tree' picture, Paul imagines the Gentiles as grafts introduced into an olive tree to replace dead branches. Our knowledge of horticulture in Paul's day is not great, but it seems that Paul is describing a process that no competent olive-grower would undertake – grafting wild shoots on to a cultivated tree. By this means Paul highlights the grace shown to the Gentiles. They do not 'belong' at all, but God has brought them in nonetheless. Just as the grafts feed on the sap of the host tree, Gentile converts are actually feeding upon Israel's covenant blessings.

This reminds us of Galatians 3, where Paul likewise tells Gentile Christians 'If you belong to Christ, then you are Abraham's seed, and heirs according to the promise' (Gal. 3:29). Gentile Christians, he insists, enter salvation by entering God's chosen people, the descendants of Abraham. They do so, however, not by becoming Jews, but by becoming united to Christ, for he is 'the seed of Abraham' in whom all the covenant promises are fulfilled (Gal. 3:16). Just as Paul's own salvation results from God's faithfulness to his people (Rom. 11:1), so does that of his Gentile converts. Later on, he justifies the efforts he devoted to raising a fund to help the Jerusalem church by saying that 'if the Gentiles have shared in the Jews' spiritual blessings, they owe it to the Jews to share with them their material blessings' (Rom. 15:27). The Gentiles' salvation is essentially Israel's, just as is the Christ himself (Rom. 9:5).

They are thus dependent upon Israel, and so should not 'boast over those [fallen] branches' (v. 18). This warning against 'boasting' is Paul's main concern in these verses. As mentioned above (pp. 120–121), he seems to have been faced not just with the Jewish-Christian position which is his main concern, but also with its Gentile-Christian opposite, namely the view that Gentiles have stepped in with the faith which Israel could not muster, and thus have displaced Israel in God's plan. He feels that this is just as grave an error, for it makes faith a 'work', and is not dependent on God's grace, but is a 'boasting'. He develops this theme:

Fear (verses 19–22)

If any Gentile Christians feel inclined to congratulate themselves on succeeding where Israel failed, then let them take heed. They stand, not by the power of their own faith, but by the 'kindness' of God. Paul attacked 'boasting' in Romans 3:27–28, and insisted that it is incompatible with faith. The man who knows himself 'justified by faith' knows also that he has nothing to boast about before God (*cf.* Rom. 4:2–3). In fact, the sight of Israel hardened in unbelief and alienated from God is an awful warning of the consequences of such 'boasting'. Gentiles must beware of falling into the same trap.

'Do not be arrogant, but be afraid!' Paul warns us. This 'fear' is perfectly compatible with rejoicing in our eternal security in Christ (Rom. 8:28ff.). The very way in which Romans 9 follows immediately after Romans 8, as we saw, shows that we cannot interpret the wonderful truth of election to mean that God writes a blank cheque for our salvation. Paul warns the Gentiles that they too, like Israel, could move from Romans 8 into Romans 9. They must 'continue in his kindness' (v. 22), which of course does not mean that they must go on earning God's kindness: rather, they must simply go on resting upon his grace, and not their own response.

Expectation (verses 23–24)

In the middle of his warning to Gentile Christians, Paul refers to Israel as 'the natural branches' (v. 21). Even fallen Israel still 'belongs' to the tree in a way in which ingrafted Gentiles never will. In the last two verses of this section, Paul picks up this point and develops it, as he continues to show that longing for Israel's restoration is not crying for the moon, but is altogether suitable and appropriate. To Gentile Christians who argued that Jews should no longer be evangelized, Paul replies that, in theory at any rate, Jews are much more likely to respond to the gospel than Gentiles. For Gentiles have to be grafted 'contrary to nature' into the tree, and so 'how much more readily will these, the natural branches, be grafted into their own olive tree?' (v. 24).

This is Paul the missionary speaking. His heart yearns for Israel's conversion, and he knows that 'God is able to graft them in again' (v. 23). Because of the form of the sentence in verse 24 ('if ... how much more ... ?'), we cannot say that he definitely predicts that God will do it. But, in answer to the question with which he began in verse 11, he has almost got as far as predicting the restoration of 'the rest'.

He has shown that the conversion of the Gentiles is God's appeal to Israel – so that she is certainly an object of his concern (vv. 11, 13f.).

He has told the Gentiles that Israel's restoration is in their own interest, because of the blessing it would bring to the world (vv. 12, 15).

He has warned the Gentiles against 'boasting' on the ground that the same could happen to them as to Israel – with the corollary that God could easily take it a stage further and bring Israel back (vv. 17–24).

He has called fallen Israel 'the natural branches', and suggested that the holiness of the root means that the branches are special too (vv. 16, 21, 24).

How much further can he go? We must remember all the time his pressing conviction that, according to Scripture, Israel is to be saved through judgment – and that right now judgment is being restrained so that the gospel may be preached world-wide (Rom. 9:22–29). During this gospel period, his own Gentile mission also focuses upon Israel, as an appeal for a change of heart. How desirable, how suitable, how right, that she should turn from her unbelief and embrace the Christ, and be grafted back into the tree of God's people!

CHAPTER FOURTEEN

God's universal purpose

[25]*I do not want you to be ignorant of this mystery, brothers, so that you may not be conceited: Israel has experienced a hardening in part until the full number of the Gentiles has come in.* [26]*And so all Israel will be saved, as it is written:*

> *'The deliverer will come from Zion;*
> *he will turn godlessness away from Jacob.*
> [27]*And this is my covenant with them*
> *when I take away their sins.'*

[28]*As far as the gospel is concerned, they are enemies on your account; but as far as election is concerned, they are loved on account of the patriarchs,* [29]*for God's gifts and his call are irrevocable.* [30]*Just as you who were at one time disobedient to God have now received mercy as a result of their disobedience,* [31]*so they too have now become disobedient in order that they too may now receive mercy as a result of God's mercy to you.* [32]*For God has bound all men over to disobedience so that he may have mercy on them all.*

> [33]*Oh, the depth of the riches of the wisdom and*
> *knowledge of God!*
> *How unsearchable his judgements,*
> *and his paths beyond tracing out!*
> [34]*'Who has known the mind of the Lord?*
> *Or who has been his counsellor?*

> [35]*'Who has ever given to God,*
> *that God should repay him?'*

³⁶*For from him and through him and to him are all things. To him be the glory for ever! Amen.*

(Romans 11:25–36)

Paul's desire to deflate 'boasting' Gentiles carries him on into this next section. In response to their denial of Israel's continuing place in God's plan, he asserts that 'all Israel will be saved' (v. 26), in fulfilment of the Old Testament (vv. 26–27), and in particular of God's promises to the patriarchs (v. 28). For, once given, God's gifts (*cf.* 9:4) and 'call' (*cf.* 9:7, 25) cannot be taken back (v. 29). In fact, he says, the Gentiles are caught up in a great undulating or interlocking movement, by which God extends salvation to them while Israel is hardened, only to reverse the process and extend mercy to Israel (vv. 30–31). Ultimately, both halves of humanity, Jews and Gentiles, are treated alike, in that both have been 'bound . . . over to disobedience' as a necessary stage on the way to receiving mercy (v. 32): the Gentiles while the tree of Israel was planted and grew, and then Israel while the Gentiles are grafted in.

Having thus outlined the 'mystery' of God's universal purpose, Paul bursts out into a hymn of praise to the Creator (vv. 33–36), focusing on his riches (v. 35), wisdom (v. 34b) and knowledge (v. 34a). In respect of all three, his ways and judgments completely surpass our capacities (v. 33b). Like Job (v. 35 quotes Job 41:11), Paul stands amazed at God's greatness. He can trace the 'what' of God's plan, but not the 'why' or the 'how'.

We want to know especially what he means by 'all Israel will be saved' (v. 26). But before reviewing the possible interpretations of this vital statement, two preliminary points must be made.

A mystery to put things right?

First, we need to consider Paul's use of the word 'mystery' in verse 25. Some scholars suggest that it changes the whole course of his argument. Up to 11:24, they say, he wrestles with the Scriptures, seeking to understand Israel's position in God's plan. But in 11:25–32 he describes the content of a special revelation, a 'mystery', which goes beyond all he could discover from Scripture. Thus, while the Old Testament spoke of judgment upon Israel and of the salvation of a remnant, this 'mystery' reveals that God in fact purposes the salvation of 'all Israel'.

Other scholars, who do not attach this special significance to 'mystery', also discern a sharp contrast between these verses and what Paul writes earlier in Romans 9 – 11. The essence of this contrast is well illustrated by the comment of one:

> It appears that the argument of 9:6–29 was almost entirely hypothetical, since the origins of Israel and God's promises to the fathers are now represented as assuring in fact the eventual salvation of the entire nation.[1]

But Knox's comment also reveals the problem with this view. Why would Paul have gone to the length of formulating his doctrine of the remnant – which he knew would provoke accusations of injustice (9:14, 19) – if he knew that in fact God was intending to save not merely a remnant, but the entire nation?

This argument also tells against the view we considered above, that Paul's emotional attachment to his own race compelled him to deny his own theology, and assert inconsistently that Israel still has a future in God's plan (see above, pp. 77–78). Romans 9:6–29 is no throw-away, hypothetical solution to the problem of Israel, rejected in favour of 'all Israel will be saved'. Whatever 11:26 means, Paul must have felt that he was drawing conclusions from his previous hard-fought argument, or he would never have undertaken it. 'Mystery' does not need to bear such weight: Paul knows he is writing of something which transcends our understanding, resting ultimately in God's plan for the whole of human

---

[1] J. Knox, *Interpreters' Bible*, vol. 9 (Abingdon, 1974), p. 571.

history (vv. 33–36), and 'mystery' is often used in such contexts (see Ephesians 1:9–11; 3:3–6, 9–10).

What sort of 'all' is 'all'?

The 'all' in 11:26 is matched by two others in 11:32, and they need to be interpreted together. In fact, verse 32 sums up the whole paragraph, looking back particularly to the balance between 'the full number of the Gentiles' and 'all Israel' in 11:25–26. When these two great masses of humanity are added together, they make the 'all men' of 11:32. But what does Paul mean, when he writes that God intends to have mercy on 'all men'?

Some commentators interpret this literally, and find a real universalism here. Paul reveals his true mind, they say: as one commentator puts it, 'In his most inspired and inspiring moments, it seems true to say, the apostle did not contemplate the final and irretrievable loss of a single soul that God has created.'[2]

If this is true, then clearly 'all Israel' will mean 'every single Jew'. It would be wonderful if this were true. And no one would have liked to believe it more than Paul himself. But if this really is what he says here, it is quite impossible to explain not only his argument in Romans 9, but also his deep expressions of grief over Israel (9:1–2; 10:1). Why should he grieve, if the problem is purely temporary, and no Jew is actually at risk? And further, if every Jew is ultimately to be saved, come what may, then Paul is in fact falling into line with his opponents, and it is completely inexplicable how and why he provoked them into such deep suspicion and hostility.

More broadly, too, a literal universalism here would contradict what he writes about the day of judgment and the reality of God's wrath in Romans 2. Difficult though these ideas may be, Paul certainly envisages the ultimate condemnation of those who 'reject the truth and follow evil' (Rom. 2:8). Such is the weight he attaches to human responsibility.

So the 'all' in 11:26, 32 must have a different force. What

---

[2] K. E. Kirk, *The Epistle to the Romans* (Oxford University Press, 1937), p. 125.

could it be? We have already received a hint in Romans 5, where Paul compared Christ and Adam, seeing them as the heads or founders of separate human races. There too he spoke of 'all men': 'Just as the result of one trespass was condemnation for all men, so also . . . [through Christ there comes] . . . justification . . . for all men' (5:18). But the 'all men' are different in each case. In the case of Adam, 'all men' is a numerical, universalist phrase, meaning 'every single human being'. But, as in 11:32, the same cannot be true of the 'all men' in Christ. And yet it is an appropriate phrase to use, for Paul presents Christ as the founder of a whole new humanity, indeed of a new creation altogther. He knows that, tragically, not 'all men' will be transferred from Adam's humanity to that of Christ. And yet we end up with a whole humanity in Christ, a saved world from which nothing is lacking.

Several other passages illustrate this distinctive way in which Paul thinks about God's universal plan: for instance, 1 Corinthians 15:21–28, Ephesians 1:10, 22f., Colossians 1:15–20. He looks at salvation from the perspective of the end, from God's point of view rather than from ours, and sees a redeemed world, a universe in which even the spiritual forces of evil (the 'principalities and powers') have been reconciled to him. But he knows, as well as we, that the road to that 'fulness' passes through the judgment and wrath of God, and he grieves deeply that Israel – bar a remnant – has fallen under that judgment, and risks ultimate loss.

Along these lines, we can see that 'all Israel' in 11:26 need not deny what Paul has previously written about Israel's experience of God's judgment. And yet we still need to discover precisely what that verse means. There are basically four ways in which it can be interpreted.

(1) 'All Israel' means 'the whole church'

This interpretation has quite a pedigree. It goes right back to the earliest centuries of Christianity, and was taken up by John Calvin the sixteenth-century Reformer: the whole church, made up of Jews and Gentiles together, will be saved – as the rightful bearer of the great covenant name 'Israel' (*cf.* Gal. 6:16).

But this cannot be right. It means taking 'Israel' in two different senses within the same sentence, for in verse 25 it plainly refers to the historic nation, and Paul drops no hints that he intends us to take it differently in verse 26. And since the whole discussion revolves around whether Israel, the historic nation, will be saved or not, in fulfilment of the covenant promises, it would actually be beside the point to assure us that the whole church will be saved. No one disputed that. No one disputed either that the church inherits the covenant blessings in Christ. But what about historic Israel, now unbelieving? This must be the 'Israel' to which Paul refers.

(2) 'All Israel' means 'the entire remnant'

A small group of scholars have supported this interpretation, which emphasizes Paul's development of the doctrine of the 'remnant' in these chapters, and argues that he is saying no more in 11:26 than he has already said in 9:27–29 or 11:5. Following the teaching of chapter 9, that God maintains his commitment to Israel by preserving a 'remnant', 11:26 simply asserts that God will continue to deal with Israel in this way. The whole remnant will be saved, and this will amount to 'all Israel' because, by definition, the 'remnant' *is* the nation, after being purified through judgment (9:27–29).

This view at least has the merit of holding together chapters 9 and 11, but it falls foul of the way in which Paul's argument develops within chapter 11. A division into saved 'remnant' and hardened 'rest' was Paul's diagnosis of Israel's present condition in 11:1–10. But from 11:11 onwards he tells us that, because of the special 'jealousy' process, we must not write 'the rest' off, and then in 11:25f. he extends that process into the future and imagines its conclusion. Israel's present 'hardening in part' is not permanent, he argues, but is only 'until the full number of the Gentiles has come in'; and then, by implication, it will end, 'and so all Israel will be saved'.

The very fact, therefore, that Paul envisages an ending of the hardening means that he believes the 'jealousy' process will work, and the remnant/rest distinction will be broken down. It is fascinating to notice that Deuteronomy 32, the chapter from which Paul develops this 'jealousy' theme, ends with a powerful divine promise of Israel's ultimate deliverance, after judgment. (Paul in fact quotes from these closing verses of Deuteronomy 32 in Romans 15:10, in the section which summarizes the whole argument of Romans.)

'All Israel' must therefore mean more than just 'the entire remnant'.

(3) 'All Israel' means 'all Jews of the last generation'

This is the favoured option among commentators on Romans and other Bible students. The conversion of the last Gentile will be followed by a huge revival among the Jews, so that all Jews then alive will be ushered into the kingdom.

There are wide variations within this interpretation. Some prefer to leave it all rather vague; others try to map out a timetable of the 'last things', including the salvation of Israel and a subsequent further revival among the Gentiles (*cf.* 11:15); for dispensationalists, the conversion of Israel marks the end of the era of the church, and the beginning of the millennial kingdom centred on Jerusalem. But all are agreed that Paul is writing of the momentous events which he feels will mark the time immediately preceding, or associated with, the second coming of Christ. This view at least has the merit of taking seriously Paul's future perspective here, but there are also great difficulties in the way of accepting it.

1. Two ways of salvation?

Dispensationalists strangely find themselves joining hands with the rather radical New Testament scholars mentioned in chapter one (see pp. 14–16). Together they argue that Paul is thinking of the fulfilment or re-instatement of the old covenant as independently valid before God. There are in fact, they say, two ways of salvation – one for Israel (the old covenant), and one for the church (the new) – and this is what Paul means when he quotes Isaiah in verse 27, 'This is my covenant with them when I take away their sins'. He is asserting that Israel will be saved because of the old covenant, the promises to the fathers which remain eternally valid alongside Christ (11:28f.).

But it would be quite impossible for the author of Romans 10 to teach this. There Paul insisted that the apostolic preaching of the gospel was absolutely essential, if 'all' – Jews and Gentiles – were to believe and be saved (10:9–15). And the theological foundation of this insistence was clear: the law has found its fulfilment in Christ (as its 'end'), so that only in him is the 'word' of the law written on the heart. Salvation through Christ is the salvation the law promised (10:4–9). This is how Paul rejected the accusation that his gospel means the annulment of the law. So how could he possibly about-turn and start teaching that the law and the old covenant have eternal, independent validity apart from Christ? If he believed this, he could not possibly have written Romans 10 as it stands. In fact, in this respect the dispensationalist view is precisely that which Paul attacks in Romans as a whole.

However the 'two ways of salvation' view is only held by a minority of those who would nonetheless support this third way of understanding 'all Israel' and 11:25–29. Most maintain that Paul envisages the salvation of the Jews through faith in Christ in 'the last days'. Yet there are further difficulties.

2. The meaning of 'and so' in 11:26

Paul uses quite an emphatic Greek phrase at the start of verse 26, translated 'and so' by NIV. Some translations give it a sense of temporal progression: the Jerusalem Bible, for instance, translates it 'and then after this', and the New English Bible paraphrases it with 'when that has happened . . .'. But the phrase simply does not mean 'and then'. It refers naturally not to the timing of Israel's salvation – after 'the fulness of the Gentiles has come in' – but to the manner of it. The Good News Bible rightly paraphrases it with, 'And this is how all Israel will be saved'.

It is important to follow the lead which Paul himself gives by his choice of words. If he had wanted to express a temporal progression from one event to another, he could easily have done so, but he chose not to. Such is the popularity of this interpretation, however, that some translations feel pushed into giving the phrase a sense which it cannot bear. We will return to this 'and so' below (see p. 157).

3. A numerical 'all'?

This view is similar to the full-blown universalist interpretation in that it gives 'all' a numerical sense, albeit limited to a particular point in time. In spite of this limitation, however, it faces the same difficulty as the universalist interpretation, in that Paul clearly does not use 'all' in a strictly numerical sense, both in this passage and elsewhere.

In this he was building upon an Old Testament practice. In 1 Samuel 12:1, for instance, 'Samuel said to all Israel' does not mean that every single Israelite then alive was standing before him in Gilgal. The body gathered there was representative of the whole, and indeed had just made a request ('Give us a king!') which gravely touched upon the whole nature of 'Israel' as God's people. Similarly in 2 Chronicles 12:1, 'He and all Israel with him abandoned the law of the Lord' does not mean that every single Jew followed Rehoboam's bad example. The author means that the apostasy of the king was such a grave matter that it could not be counter-balanced by the remaining faithful: in essence, 'all Israel' had gone astray, such was the importance of the king both theologically and socially.

In other words, the fact that Paul writes 'all Israel' and not 'all Jews' is significant, as we shall see.

4. Does Isaiah 59:20–21 refer to the second coming?

This is the passage Paul quotes in verses 26–27, adding a line from Isaiah 27:9. Those who support this 'all Jews of the end' interpretation tend to attach the quotation just to verse 26a, and to take it as a prophecy of Christ's second coming: when he comes again, it will be especially to deliver Israel from her 'hardening in part', to 'turn godlessness away from Jacob', so that 'all Israel will be saved'. But there are clear reasons against applying the quotation in this way.

First, Paul has deliberately altered the quotation, so as to make it apply to verse 25 as well. Isaiah 59:20 promises that a Redeemer will come 'to' Zion (*i.e.* Jerusalem, Israel): Paul changes 'to' to 'from', thus importing into Isaiah the idea of the blessing and 'coming-in' of the Gentiles, expressed in verse 25. He uses Isaiah to express the relationship between the two salvations: the coming of the Redeemer 'from' Zion is set alongside his 'turning away of godlessness from Jacob', just as the coming in of the fulness of the Gentiles (v. 25) is co-ordinated with the salvation of Israel (v. 26). They turn out to be the two poles of one mighty act of redemption.

But this alteration shows that Paul is not thinking of the second coming of Christ. It is in the present age, following his first coming, that the gospel goes out 'from Zion' to the Gentiles – indeed, it was Paul's insistence on this which caused all the trouble. By definition, the Gentiles will no longer need a Redeemer, after their 'fulness' has come in. This means, logically, that 'turning away godlessness from Jacob' is also something that follows from Christ's first coming, rather than from his second. (We must not be misled by the future tense, 'will come . . . will turn'. It is future from Isaiah's standpoint, not from Paul's.)

This is an interesting feature of the way Paul quotes the Old Testament. Quite frequently he changes it in order to make it express the thought he wants to draw out of it. We have already seen small examples of this in his addition of 'all' to the quotation of Isaiah in 10:11, and in his alteration of 1 Kings 19:18 in 11:4. Some scholars throw up their hands in horror, and criticize Paul for misusing the Old Testament. But the fascinating thing is that he never imports an idea into a text which is really foreign to it, something which would really have been contrary to its original intention. Some have charged him with doing this in Romans 10:6–8, but (as we saw) the charge is ill-founded.

Interestingly, his addition of 'all' in 10:11 has the same force as his insertion of 'from' here: both of them add the thought, so frequently found in Isaiah, that God intends to bless and draw in the Gentiles through his blessing of Israel. We have also noticed how Paul likes to combine verses into composite quotations, as in 11:8, where three separate texts are joined. The process illustrated by his addition of 'from' in 11:26 is an extension of the same technique, whereby not just texts but also ideas are combined from different places.

Romans 11:26 also illustrates another aspect of Paul's 'free' use of the Old Testament. The Hebrew of Isaiah 59:20 actually reads, 'The Redeemer will come . . . to those in Jacob who turn from their sins'. Paul quotes from the Septuagint, the Greek translation of the Old Testament, which in this case is a mistranslation. Paul was, of course, deeply familiar with the Hebrew Old Testament, and will have been well aware of the mistake in the Septuagint. But he retains it – again, because it expresses a thoroughly good Old Testament idea, albeit not one native to that verse.

So the 'freedom' with which Paul quoted the Old Testament did not allow him to distort it in his favour. It was really a freedom to cut corners in presentation, and so to make us work harder to follow the rapid train of his thought!

Secondly, we may comment more broadly that, whenever Paul writes of the second coming elsewhere, he thinks of judgment, not of redemption. Romans 11:26f. would be very unusual, as a reference to a work of redemption from sin carried out by Christ at the end. Verses like 1 Corinthians 15:24f., 2 Corinthians 5:10 and 1 Thessalonians 5:1–3 give Paul's usual emphasis: 'While people are saying "Peace and safety", destruction will come on them suddenly . . .' (1 Thes. 5:3). This makes it much more likely that Paul is not thinking of the second coming in Romans 11:26f.

5. What about the 'now' in verse 31b?

The NIV quite rightly includes a second 'now' in verse 31. Many other translations – for instance, NEB and RSV – simply omit it. But it has a dramatic effect on the meaning. Speaking of the outworking of the 'jealousy' process over the whole span of God's plan, Paul writes, 'they too [*i.e.* Israel] have now become disobedient in order that they too may now receive mercy as a result of God's mercy to you'.

It is quite true that not all manuscripts of Romans include this second 'now'. But some of the earliest and best manuscripts do include it, and it is clear that the scribes who copied out the New Testament felt some embarrassment about it.

Some of them put in 'later', in order perhaps to deliver Paul from having made a false prophecy. Some simply left it out, perhaps for the same reason, while others faithfully retained it.

The argument is definitely on the side of including this second 'now'. If Paul did indeed write it, it becomes even more difficult to maintain the 'Jews of the end' interpretation of 11:26.

These arguments amount to a cogent case against this 'standard' interpretation of 'all Israel'. But if Paul is not predicting the mass conversion of Israel at the end of the age, what is he saying? This brings us to the fourth possibility.

(4) 'All Israel' means 'all elect Israelites'

This is clearly the direction in which our journey through Paul's argument has been leading. His first step towards an answer to the problem of Israel's apostasy was to argue that 'not all who are descended from Israel are Israel' (9:6). He restricted the applicability of the name 'Israel' to the group he calls 'the children of the promise' (9:8), and then developed a doctrine of election within the nation in order to argue that God's 'word' to Israel is fulfilled even now, in her apostasy (9:10–29). This is also the thrust of 11:1–10.

So we begin to understand 'all Israel' in 11:26 when we realize that 'Israel' bears the sense Paul gave it in 9:6: the 'Israel' that truly bears the 'promise', which is an 'Israel' to be distinguished from 'all Jews'. In our wrestling with Romans 9, we have already sought to come to terms with this understanding of election.

At the same time, however, Paul has clearly suggested that God yet has more in store than Israel's present apostasy suggests. Even though there is nothing in the present situation to support an accusation that God has not kept his word, yet Paul believed that he was holding back the execution of his wrath, because Hosea's vision of the re-calling of the people was not yet fulfilled (9:22–26). Developing this, Paul suggests in 11:11–24 that the distinction between 'the remnant' (who have obtained salvation) and 'the rest' (who have been hardened) is not final: he still longs and works for the salvation of 'some' through 'envy' (11:14), and he thinks of the present-day remnant as the 'firstfruits', conveying an idea of the 'holiness' of the rest of the people (11:16).

As we saw above (pp. 150–151), it is this development of his argument in 11:11–24 which undermines the 'entire remnant' interpretation of 'all Israel'. Paul must mean more than the 'remnant', because his argument has moved on from that point. He uses the 'remnant' idea in order to combine the ideas of salvation and judgment: the 'remnant' is that which 'remains' after judgment, and therefore always has that flavour mixed into it (11:4). So the remnant exists 'at the present time' (11:5), in the midst of a generation on which judgment has been pronounced (11:8). But the 'envy' principle, on the other hand, points into the future, and means that Paul can hope for the salvation even of 'the rest' – or at any rate 'some of them' (11:14).

But moving beyond the 'remnant' idea does not mean that Paul abandons the thought of election within the people. This is basic to his whole argument. The remnant is a particular manifestation of a principle which operates throughout God's dealings with Israel, not just at points of judgment: he 'has mercy on whom he wants to have mercy, and he hardens whom he wants to harden' (9:18). The assurance given to Hosea, that 'I will call them "my people" who are not my people' (9:25), does not set aside this principle of election within Israel, but expresses it. Paul sees it being fulfilled in the 'calling' of the church from the Jews (and from the Gentiles – 9:24). 'All Israel' in 11:26, I believe, is the entire company of those 'from the Jews' whom God wills to call 'my people', in fulfilment of his purposes of election. This interpretation avoids the difficulties of the others, and allows 11:25ff. to be the natural completion of the argument of all three chapters.

'And so . . .'

The 'mystery' which Paul wants his Gentile readers to grasp (11:25) is to do with the manner in which God will fulfil this purpose. In fact, this is the point to which his argument has been leading. He could have stopped at the end of chapter 9, if he had simply wanted to argue that 'the elect' were a smaller group than all the descendants of Abraham, and that only the 'children of promise' could rightly bear the name 'Israel'. What has been impelling Paul through chapters 10 and 11, as we have seen, has been the inclusion of the Gentiles, or rather the relationship between Israel and the Gentiles in God's plan. Now that train of thought reaches a climax, with the 'and so' at the beginning of verse 26.

We have already seen how this 'and so' cannot mean 'and then'. Rather, we should paraphrase it with, 'and so, in this way'. Paul is thinking of a process which produces the result he then specifies – the salvation of all Israel. This process he describes in verse 25: 'Israel has experienced a hardening in part until the "fulness" [NIV: "full number"] of the Gentiles has come in'. What exactly does he mean?

'The fulness of the Gentiles' is clearly the point at which God's plan of salvation for the Gentile world has been completed. The 'coming in' of this fulness is not a great event in itself, but merely the completion of something which has been long growing and developing. NIV is not alone in giving 'fulness' a basically numerical flavour. Other translations do the same: 'full strength' (NEB, Phillips), 'full inclusion' (RSV), 'complete number' (GNB), 'conversion of them all' (Jerusalem Bible). This idea of the 'full number' is probably correct, although the word naturally suggests a wider meaning. Paul uses the same word with reference to Israel in 11:12, where he makes it the opposite of 'transgression' and 'loss' (there, NIV translates it 'fulness'). Probably in both verses it carries the idea of being brought to perfection, in addition to the idea of the 'full number' of the elect whom God intends to 'call'.

At any rate, the Gentiles move towards this fulness while a 'hardening in part' rests upon Israel. Paul clearly still has the 'envy' process basically in mind, although he seems to have developed it a little. Instead of saying that the blessing of the Gentiles results from Israel's wilful rebellion and is an appeal for her repentance, he suggests that Israel's hardening has been purposed, in order that the Gentiles may be brought in. This is certainly the way in which he pictures it in 11:30: NIV has mistranslated here(I believe), by putting the phrase 'as a result of God's mercy to you' at the end of verse 31. It should be attached to the start: '. . . so they too have now become disobedient as a result of God's mercy to you . . .'. Somehow, the disobedience of Israel was necessary, for the sake of the Gentiles. She has been 'hardened in part': the 'in part' arises from the existence of the present-day remnant, to which Paul belongs, who show that Israel has not been totally hardened.

But this hardening will only last as long as the reason for its existence still holds: 'until the fulness of the Gentiles comes in'. Then it will end. Paul is using broad brush-strokes here, and perhaps we can trace the fine lines of the picture in the following way. Every time a Gentile turns to faith in Christ, his conversion arises out of Israel's unbelief, and constitutes an appeal, a testimony from God, to Jews who notice it. Every time a Jew turns to faith in Christ, his conversion means that the appeal has been heeded, and constitutes a lessening of the hardening upon Israel (the hardened 'part' is smaller by one). Both processes continue side-by-side, with the lines gradually converging, as (on the one hand) the fulness of the Gentiles draws near and thus the reason for Israel's hardening approaches fulfilment, and (on the other hand) the hardening grows less and less as more and more Jews are made 'jealous' and believe. As Paul projects the 'jealousy' principle into the future, he foresees a point at which the two lines will meet – when simultaneously the hardening of Israel will end, and the fulness of the Gentiles will be complete. It must be simultaneous, because each half of the process has been dependent on the other half.

'And so, in this way, all Israel will be saved': this is the manner in which God has determined to call his people to himself, to save the 'children of promise' who make up 'Israel'. The Deliverer who has come from Zion out into the Gentile world, by that very coming also turns godlessness away from Jacob (v. 26b): the blessing of the Gentiles is the cause and the occasion both of Israel's unbelief and disobedience, and of Israel's ultimate salvation.

When?

Does Paul give any indication of the timing of all this? If, as I argued above, (a) 'the Deliverer will come from Zion' (v. 26b) refers to the first coming of Christ, and (b) the second 'now' should be kept in verse 31, then 'all Israel will be saved' is the only directly future statement in the passage. Some scholars have suggested that we should think twice before reading the passage of centuries into Paul's language here: his perspective is short-term. Some have even linked this passage to Paul's forthcoming journey to Jerusalem, bearing the gifts of the Gentile churches (15:25–27), and have argued that he saw this as possibly the 'fulness of the Gentiles', and was hoping for the conversion of Israel through it.

In favour of this theory, we can point to 11:13–14 where, as we saw, his Jerusalem visit fits into his desire to 'glorify' his ministry in order to provoke Jews to jealousy (see above, p. 139). Undoubtedly, he was hoping that the process he pictures in 11:25 would move along a little, as a result of his visit. But on the other hand, he was busily making plans for further missionary activity among the Gentiles *after* his trip to Jerusalem (15:28–29). He clearly did not expect the salvation of 'all Israel' so soon, because (at the very least) he felt he had to take the gospel to Spain before 'the fulness of the Gentiles' could come in (15:28). In accordance with his view, the blessing which he expects to experience among the Romans when he visits them (15:29), will itself arise out of Israel's hardening, and will constitute a strengthening of God's appeal to her.

So he gives no indication of the 'when' of Israel's salvation. This means that we may share his hope and expectation. Just as he was convinced that God had called him to be apostle to the Gentiles, so he was sure, because of that very call, that there would be spiritual fruit among Jews as well, matching that among the Gentiles. He thinks of the two great halves of humanity, Israel and the Gentiles, as gradually moving towards a great complementary fulfilment, each bound up with the other. 'The fulness of the Gentiles' balances 'all Israel will be saved' (vv. 25–26), and together they make up the 'all men' whom God has 'bound . . . over to disobedience so that he may have mercy on them all' (11:32).

We may have the same confidence today, in spite of all the horrors of Christian maltreatment of the Jews over the centuries. On the face of it, we have done the very opposite of provoking them to 'jealousy'. But Paul rests his confidence on God's plan and purpose, and we may do the same. He had to work hard to convince his Gentile churches of the need to contribute to his collection for the Jerusalem church (see, *e.g.*, 2 Corinthians 8). Even then, the pressures driving them apart were great. But Paul refused to give in to these pressures, as he looked beyond the actual historical circumstances of his ministry to God's plan for the world and saw it as one purpose, joining together Jews and Gentiles in the one 'tree' of the covenant, through Christ. So he fought to hold Jews and Gentiles together within the church, and to convey to his Gentile converts a sense of their indebtedness to Israel. From all this we may learn for today. In the next chapter, we will reflect briefly on what this may mean in practice.

Worship his majesty

So Paul reaches a perspective on the divine plan in which even rejection and disobedience serve God's plan of salvation. First the Gentiles stood outside the orbit of the covenant, while Israel was chosen and blessed ('you who were at one time disobedient', v. 30a). But the purpose of Israel's election was so that the world might be blessed; so now Israel's apostasy (in part) is the occasion of the world-wide extension of the covenant blessings ('you . . . have now received mercy as a result of their disobedience', v. 30b). But this incorporation of undeserving Gentiles into the people of God is to lead in turn to the regrafting of the fallen branches ('. . . in order that they too may now receive mercy', v. 31b). The result will be a saved world, in which God's plan has been brought to perfect completion. His word has not fallen.

No wonder Paul finishes these chapters with a paean of praise to the God whose 'unsearchable judgments' surpass our capacity to grasp. He carefully incorporates two Old

Testament quotations into the little hymn in 11:33–36: Isaiah 40:13 in verse 34, and Job 41:11 in verse 35. Both suit his purpose, in more ways than one. First, the three rhetorical questions formed by these quotations pick up in turn the three qualities of God on which Paul focuses his praise in verse 33 – in reverse order. 'Who has known the mind of the Lord?' praises his knowledge. 'Who has been his counsellor?' praises his wisdom. And 'Who has ever given to God, that God should repay him?' praises his riches. All the resources are his, to achieve whatever his heart desires or his wisdom plans.

Secondly, both verses arise in similar situations. Isaiah sought to understand the providence of a God who promised an everlasting commitment to Israel, while sending her into exile and apparently abandoning her. Job wrestled likewise with an inscrutable wisdom which decreed suffering, deprivation and death as part of a perfect ordering of his servants' circumstances. Paul knows that he has been facing precisely the same problem, and that the answer is the same too. He reaches, with Job, the point at which he confesses wonderment for what he can understand, and adoration for what he cannot.

CHAPTER FIFTEEN

Christians and Jews today

Our journey through Romans 9 – 11 is complete. In conclusion, we ask, What would Paul say to us today, if he
stood in our position, looking back over the 2,000 years
of separation, mistrust, hatred and persecution which is the
history of Christian-Jewish relationships (lightened only by
an occasional gleam of true charity)?

Some things we may take for granted. He would certainly
tell us to repent, and to replace indifference and hostility with
love. Though hated by many of his fellow-Jews, he never
ceased loving them. Although, thankfully, the church of the
present generation stands back from the sins of the past, we
are yet in inevitable solidarity with our fathers in the faith
who had such a blind spot towards Israel. We must repent
for what they did, in so far as this is possible. And we must
seek to give our repentance concrete forms.

Paul would also tell us to become aware of our roots – and
this might be one of the ways of making repentance real. Jesus
was a Jew, as Paul was. He believed that his Gentile converts
had been admitted on to Israel's holy ground. Even in writing
to converts with a purely pagan background, he filled his
letters with Old Testament quotations and allusions, in a way
which must have conveyed this thought to them vividly. Even
the Holy Communion, the heart of Christian worship, cannot
be understood apart from its Old Testament and Jewish background. And yet, in the church today, many Christians are
not only unaware of the historical roots of their faith, but are
also lamentably ignorant of the Old Testament, and regard

it as foreign to their concerns. This is tragic.

But I believe Paul would tell us to beware of emotional attachment. I am deeply impressed by the way in which his head ruled his heart. His feelings for his own nation, so movingly expressed in Romans 9:1–2 and 10:1, would have impelled lesser thinkers to a theology which gave rest to a tortured spirit. But the Scriptures were supreme for him – even to the extent of comparing Israel to Sodom. We too need to beware. In fact, it is possible for Gentile Christians to be more emotionally attached than many Jews to the thought of Israel's special position in God's plan. Paul would tell us to keep a check on our desires, and to submit everything to the test of Scripture.

But if we may take these things for granted, what else can we see, arising particularly out of our study of Romans 9 – 11? We will tackle this question, first from a basically negative perspective – what Paul would not support or encourage – and then from a positive. We are aided in this by the remarkable fact that, as we have seen, the practical situation which Paul was facing in Romans raised the very questions to which we want answers today.

Paul would not be happy about . . .

1. The view that Israel has her own way of salvation, or that Jews should not be 'evangelized'

The Sisters of Sion (see above, p. 12) believe that the Holy Spirit has led them to this view, in development of some of the pointers Paul gives. But Paul cannot be interpreted as 'pointing' to a position diametrically opposed to his own, for this position is totally at variance with the message of Romans 9 – 11. He believed that salvation was only to be found in Christ, that the apostolic ministry of gospel proclamation was the fulfilment of the law, and that Israel would only be delivered from 'godlessness' as she was provoked by 'jealousy' into faith in Christ. We may find this uncomfortable today, but it was just as uncomfortable for Paul. Of course, there is much that may be said about the kind of evangelism appropriate in the case of the Jews, and Paul will lead us here too (see below, pp. 169–172), but undoubtedly this is what he would tell us, in principle. His 'great sorrow and unceasing anguish' over Israel's unbelief (Rom. 9:2) is completely inexplicable on this showing.

2. The view that Israel constitutes the 'centre of God's plan' for the world

The olive-tree simile in Romans 11:17–24 presents Israel as the centre of God's plan, in one sense: Paul tells the Gentile believers to think of themselves as joined by grace to God's historic people, feeding on Israel's 'nourishing sap' (v. 17). But I do not believe that he would be happy with this view as taught in dispensationalist or other prophetic schemes, or even as maintained by scholars like T. F. Torrance (see above, p. 16). If Paul had believed anything like this, then with one or two words he could have put his opponents' minds at rest and spared himself a great deal of trouble. Romans 9 becomes inexplicable. Why should he wrestle to define and defend a theology of election within Israel, including those stunningly stark statements which must have provoked even greater ire from his opponents, if he believed in fact that nothing could challenge Israel's supremacy among the nations, as his opponents conceived it?

For let us not be mistaken: the understanding of the Jewish people held by many contemporary 'Israel' theologians is essentially that of Paul's opponents. They probably spoke for a majority of Jewish Christians in condemning Paul's law-free Gentile mission, because they all felt that he demoted Israel from her central place among the nations by such a mission. The law guaranteed this position to her.

The setting has changed today, and different garnishes have been added around the sides. It is no longer possible to argue that a law-free Gentile church is wrong in principle; the various prophetic schemes into which Israel is slotted give the whole thing a different appearance; and history, especially in the twentieth century, inevitably shapes the way we think about the Jews today. But at its heart, the view that Israel is the centre of the divine purpose in the world is precisely the view that Paul opposed, for this position belongs to Christ. From now on, he insisted, the law finds validity only in him who is its 'end', and the people of the law likewise find their destiny only as they are bound up with the world-wide people of the Christ. Again, it is a hard message, both then and now. But if Paul had believed otherwise, he would have said so.

3. The view that Israel has completely lost all distinctive significance in God's plan

Some Christians would say a hearty 'Amen' to what I have just written, and take it to imply that the distinction between 'Israel' and 'the Gentiles' has been wholly abolished through Christ.

But such is the subtlety of Paul's position, that he would have nothing of this either. His opponents accused him of teaching this, but he rejected the accusation vigorously, and opposed the Gentile Christians who did teach it. As we have seen, he carefully treads a middle path. Nothing can change the fact that Israel first received the word of promise – the word through which all men are now saved in Christ. God will keep his covenant with Israel, although we cannot tell him how to keep it. But to reject the election of Israel is to reject God's word and thus to undermine faith in the Christ, who comes to us in fulfilment of God's promises and cannot be understood apart from them. This is something which needs to be said with equal emphasis today, for dispensation-alism and its companion theologies can produce a backlash amongst Christians who want to have nothing to do with such schemes, and throw out the baby (Israel) with the bathwater. We need Paul's delicacy.

Romans 11:25–32 needs to be interpreted carefully in the light of Paul's whole argument, as we have seen. But no-one can properly read those verses and conclude that, for Paul, Israel no longer figures in God's plan. We will think further below about the positive side of this (see p. 172).

4. The view that the establishment of the State of Israel, and the return of Jews to their homeland, are a literal fulfilment of prophecy

We are on less sure ground here, for we have not undertaken a full discussion of the competing claims of 'literal' and 'spiritual' interpretations of Old Testament prophecy. But we have seen Paul using prophecy in the course of his argument in Romans 9 – 11, and to judge from his treatment of it I believe he would not be happy with the 'literal' application of Old Testament texts to these events.

It is worth remembering that Jews were scattered all over the known world in Paul's day also. A literal interpretation of the prophecies of regathering was open to him too. He quotes from only one passage concerned with the return from exile in Romans 9 – 11, but this is sufficient to suggest clearly what his approach was. Deuteronomy 30 sets the 'circumcision of heart' (which Paul feels has come about in Christ, Rom. 10:6–9) in the context of a restoration of Israel to the Promised Land after judgment: see above, pp. 101–105. Paul takes the prophecy seriously, and delights in it. But he clearly feels that it has already been fulfilled through Christ, even with the Jews scattered over the world.

The reason is not hard to find. He applies the prophecy to Gentiles, as well as to Jews, for he believes that Gentiles are being brought in to enjoy Israel's blessings. But they enjoy them by grace, not by law: and we could translate this vital principle and add that they enjoy them by the Spirit and not by the flesh, in the heart and not through the letter, in Christ and not in a special place. All these things go together for Paul. And this is not a special concession for Gentiles: he is saying that this is how the promise of restoration is to be fulfilled for Jews, also.

He gives a spiritual interpretation to other verses, too, which we might have expected him to interpret literally if he were inclined that way: Joel 2:32 (Rom. 10:13) and Isaiah 59:20 (Rom. 11:26) come especially to mind. In both cases he feels they have been fulfilled already, in the coming of Christ, even with Israel still in a state of unbelief.

So it looks as though he would urge us to be very cautious about finding the fulfilment of Old Testament prophecies in events other than the life, death and resurrection of Christ. He is, after all, the end of the law. He is the people of God in person (see Gal. 3:19, 26–29), and all are invited to enjoy God's blessings in him, not in Israel.

5. The use of the title 'the people of God' to refer to the Jews

It all depends, of course, on precisely what is meant when the Jews are called 'the people of God' today. But often it is used with the unspoken sense, 'the people of God still, as in Old Testament times'. I do not believe that Paul would be happy with this, even though he certainly finds it proper to speak of the Jews as 'the people of God'.

Now that Christ has come, nothing can be 'as in Old Testament times'. For Paul, everything has become relative to Christ, and this is the consistently Christian position. He knows that 'people of God' is the great Old Testament title for Israel, and uses it as such several times in Romans (9:25; 10:21; 11:1; 15:10). But because the Gentiles have stumbled upon the 'righteousness of God' in Christ, Paul is happy to apply the title to the church, made up of Jews and Gentiles together (Rom. 9:25–26, quoting Hosea: see above, pp. 75–77). Israel is still God's people in the sense that nothing can alter history, and therefore she was, and still is, the recipient of God's glorious promises, which he will certainly keep. But in the fuller sense, the title is now borne by the church, which enters into the reality of being 'sons of the living God'.

Having said this, however, it is important to note that Paul does not often apply 'people of God' to the church – perhaps because of its close association with Israel the nation. In addition to Romans 9:25f., he only does so elsewhere in 2 Corinthians 6:16 (*cf.* also Tit. 2:14).

Having looked at the negative side, we turn to the positive, and ask:

How should we actively respond to Paul's vision of Israel?

I believe there are three ways in which Paul would urge Christians today to shape their faith and practice, in order to give expression to his vision of Israel.

1. 'To the Jew first – and also to the Greek'

This is Paul's own phrase, used three times in Romans (1:16; 2:9, 10) in a way that teasingly anticipates his argument in chapters 9 – 11. We can imagine Gentile readers scratching their heads over that 'first', and Jews over the 'and also'. Paul seemed to be trying to have it both ways at once. By the time he gets to the end of Romans 11, Paul hopes that he has justified this programme. Of course, it is the gospel which goes 'to the Jew first' (Rom. 1:16).

Time has not altered the validity of the arguments by which he establishes his 'to the Jew first' (which, as we saw, reflects his own missionary practice of preaching first in the synagogue in each place). Nothing has altered the list of blessings in Romans 9:3–4. They still 'belong' to Israel by 'nature' (Rom. 11:24), and it is still as great a tragedy that she has not entered into the real enjoyment of them, in Christ.

We do Jews small service by communicating to them simply our awareness of the roots of our own faith in theirs, and our appreciation of their cultural heritage. Their heritage is great indeed: but Paul's awareness of it simply deepened his longing that they should be saved through Christ. He is close to us, in that for him too the centre of gravity had shifted out into the Gentile world. But even so he understood his Gentile ministry only in relation to Israel (Rom. 11:13–14). Has the passage of time altered this?

I believe that Christian mission amongst the Jews should receive priority on the list of Christian concerns. This view is rather contrary to the climate of the times, and it may be that the word 'mission' is not the best one to use. In a booklet entitled 'Dialogue and Proclamation – Paralysis of Confidence', Walter Riggans discusses the whole question of 'mission' to Israel, and notes the way in which many of the words used to refer to it, such as 'proselytizing', 'evangelism', 'conversion', and 'witnessing', now have bad flavours attached to them, because of the insensitive and arrogant way in which Christians have preached at Jews in the past. He quotes the words of J. G. Davies, 'Monologue is entirely lacking in humility', and suggests that a sensitive combination of 'dialogue' and 'witness' is the right approach:

> Our testimony to Jesus as Israel's Messiah has a rhythmic quality as it moves graciously and purposefully between the *retrospective* movement of learning and listening about God and our faith from Israel, and the *prospective* movement of witnessing to Israel about our God and our faith.
> (p. 11, the italics are his emphasis)

Much care needs to be devoted to the attitude with which such a witness is undertaken. Paul gives us guidelines here too, which we will consider next. Here we simply note the principle: if Paul were applying the message of Romans 9 – 11 today, he would certainly support the rightness of testimony about Jesus. And Walter Riggans suggests a helpful framework within which such a testimony can be given, by his combination of retrospective dialogue and prospective witness. It means, on the one hand, looking back into the past, to review, rediscover and repent, seeking new understanding with total openness; while also looking forward into the future and bearing humble witness to the Christ who holds all things and all mankind in his hands, and invites us to fellowship with him.

In fact, few Gentile Christians may be called directly to this kind of ministry among Jews, but the care and the prayer which so burdened Paul's heart (Rom. 10:1) is within reach of all of us. How aware are we of the Old Testament foundations upon which our faith rests? How conscious are we that it is the God of Abraham, Isaac and Jacob to whom we pray? Do we see the window opened into God's heart by the words of Jesus, 'I was sent only to the lost sheep of Israel'

(Mt. 15:24)? Our Christian faith will not be true to itself, until it becomes aware in this way, and begins to beat to this pulse, and starts to feel the tragedy of a Messiah unrecognized.

2. 'I magnify my ministry, hoping to make my kinsmen jealous and save some of them' (Rom. 11:13–14)

We have seen how vital this idea of 'jealousy' is for Paul's whole theory of the place of Israel in God's plan. It also contains vital guidance as we take forward the last point and ask, How can Christian witness to Jews be preserved from the pitfalls of 'monologue' (see above), and be conducted with genuine openness and love?

Two points arise from Paul's words here. First, 'I magnify my ministry' points to a process whereby he hopes that Jews will simply see the blessings poured out on the Gentiles – in fact, 'the righteousness of God' resting upon them – and be prompted to want it for themselves. The actual, discernible moral transformation of his Gentile converts, by the Holy Spirit, was vital for Paul, and lies at the heart of his 'jealousy' theory.

This means, for us, that our whole lifestyle as Christians will be a vital part of our testimony – perhaps the major part – before ever we open our mouths to speak of Jesus. Unless Jews see in us a quality inexplicable apart from the grace of God, then our words will fall on deaf ears. In particular, unless they see in Christians the compelling love of God's people, a community life which is deeper and more attractive even than that found in many Jewish communities, they will never be convinced. It is our lack of love towards Jews which is so particularly shaming – that we who claim the Spirit of God have so signally failed to love the people God loves.

Secondly, Paul's use of 'some of them' is important. He was not expecting mass conversions among the Jews through his witness – rather, one here and another there. Today too, Christian witness among the Jews will proceed best on a personal basis. 'Mass evangelism' is hardly likely to be an appropriate method here. Only in the context of genuine

171

friendship can dialogue be joined to witness, because mutual trust is needed to prevent false motives and misunderstandings.

3. 'And so all Israel will be saved' (Rom. 11:26)

We need to maintain the vision that inspired Paul.

As we have seen, the fulfilment of God's plan for Israel was right at the heart of his plan for the world, as Paul saw it. He could not conceive of the one without the other. In this sense Israel really is at the centre of God's plan – in that hers is the Christ through whom all men are saved. God's covenant with her will be completely fulfilled, because it is through that covenant, and no other, that the whole world is saved. If the gospel is to run its course, if every knee is one day to bow at the name of Jesus, then Israel must be saved, for it will be the promise of salvation made to her which will be fulfilled on that great day. No-one is ever saved, except by becoming a child of Abraham – in Christ.

This is the vision that inspired Paul, and it should be ours too. More than anything else, I believe, Paul would want us to transform our attitude towards the Jews. Even in the post-Auschwitz age, Christians generally live in ignorance and negligence of them. Paul would encourage us to attitudes of repentance, prayer, heartfelt longing, humble witness and fervent hope. For we do not just remind ourselves that God can graft the 'natural branches' back in, if he so wills; we are also aware that he *must* do so, if his promises are to be fulfilled – and therefore that he *will* do so, according to his unsearchable wisdom, so that on the day of Christ all humanity in both its halves will be there to confess that 'Jesus Christ is Lord, to the glory of God the Father!' (Phil. 2:11).